CONTENTS

Introduction

Who fears to speak of the Easter Rising?

How should we remember the Irish rebels who stormed the GPO 100 years ago and launched an uprising against British rule? Ireland, it seems, is a country divided not just by partition, but by a clash of opinions on how this seminal event should be commemorated.

One section of the political class, led by figures such as former Taoiseach John Bruton, argue that we should be ashamed and feel guilty. From this perspective, the Rising put the gun into Irish politics. It gave birth to political violence and damaged the Irish psyche. Such a view finds no shortage of friends with similar assessments in the pages of Ireland's biggest-selling paper the *Irish Independent* and in the establishment paper the *Irish Times*. Perhaps such a view should come as no real surprise, as both papers expressed a similar editorial sentiment a century ago in the days following the Easter Rising.

From this perspective, the centenary is surely no time for celebration – quite the opposite in fact. The event itself is seen as an act of armed rebellion by an extremist group outside the mainstream of nationalist politics with no electoral mandate. It is viewed with disdain, all the more so because the United Kingdom of Great Britain and Ireland was in all-out war with Germany. In case you are unclear about how treacherous the rebels were, we are reminded that the Great War had the overwhelming support of Ireland's democratically elected representatives to the UK Parliament and that the leaders of the rebellion had sought and received aid from Germany.

Dennis Kennedy, former deputy editor of the *Irish Times*, captured well the attitude of those hostile to the Rising. Writing in the *Irish Times* on how we should approach the centenary commemoration, he described the rebels as: 'Ideologues with no electoral support, prepared to kill and destroy in pursuit of their political aims'. He went on:

The long shadow of the gunman of 1916 has helped inspire IRA campaigns in practically every decade since 1922, and still does today.[1]

A less overtly hostile view is expressed by the Irish government when marking the centenary. However, what comes across is not enthusiasm and admiration when looking back on the Rising, but ambiguity tinged with embarrassment. How else would one assess the now infamous 80-second promotional video titled 'Ireland Inspires 2016', released to coincide with the launch of the official 2016 centenary programme at the GPO? Vacuous and banal, the film was a comedy-sketch writer's dream. In a video that features poets, U2, Bob Geldof, The Queen of England, David Cameron and various sports stars, at no point are Patrick Pearse, James Connolly or indeed any of the other 1916 leaders mentioned. In an act of sycophantic flattery aimed at the corporate and global business world, the video features references to the social media companies Facebook and LinkedIn, both of which have established operation in Ireland in recent years.

There is nothing wrong with giving positive endorsement to multinational companies and signalling that your country is open for business if that is what you are into. However, in an 80-second video launching the official commemoration of the Easter Rising, this is bizarre. No wonder outraged relatives of those who fought in the Easter Rising described government commemoration plans as a joke. Producing a centenary piece that shows Queen Elizabeth, David Cameron, Enda Kenny and Ian Paisley, but not Patrick Pearse and James Connolly nor even a single mention of the Rising or any figure involved, tells us something. It indicates a nervousness and reluctance on the part of those in power to embrace the motives, ideas and people of the Easter Rising. Rather than remembering the founding of a nation, they preferred to produce what looks like a Bórd Fáilte (Irish Tourist Board) video mixed with a promotional film pitching for economic investment overseas. Satirists call it the 'Don't Mention the War' video.

One does not have to agree with the John Brutons and Dennis Kennedys of this world, but at least they are honest and forthright in their condemnation of the Easter Rising and its legacy. On the other hand, Taoiseach Enda Kenny and those in control of the Centenary Celebrations have acted in bad faith. They talk in doublespeak and clichés. Their energy is not directed at genuinely exploring or celebrating the legacy of the Rising but rather controlling it. They are hostile to any spontaneous and grass-roots expression of Irish nationalism outside of their control and have tried desperately to sanitise and neuter the widespread involvement of ordinary people in the Centenary Celebrations.

The government's attitude mirrors the fear of popular nationalism and contempt for ordinary people found in elites across Europe; these are the kind of people more comfortable conferencing with other world leaders than with the demands of their own people.

The notorious video 'Ireland Inspires', now quietly dropped after howls of protest, is a metaphor for a managerialist breed of politics which is the antithesis of just about everything the republicans of 1916 stood for. Today's Irish government practices a type of elite politics not only aloof from ordinary people, but also a million miles removed from radical ideas contained in the proclamation read out on the steps of the GPO 100 years ago.

The Easter Rising, born of political violence, gave birth to the independent nation state over which Kenny governs, yet his political class writhes uncomfortably at any mention of real sovereignty as expressed by those who fought and died for it in 1916. No doubt they would love to cast a spell visiting a collective amnesia over the nation so they could move on and cosy up to the Brussels elite, safe in the notion of never having to account for how the Republic of Ireland's independence was won or what genuine sovereignty means. This political class is embarrassed by 1916 but most are afraid to say so publically, hence they practice the politics of ambiguity and dishonest historical revision as a way of avoiding the truth and real debate.

An example of such bad faith and deceit was the report from the British-Irish Parliamentary assembly, warning against 'triumphalist' celebrations of the centenary of the Easter Rising lest they encourage violence and tension. In a staggering piece of myth-making, these British and Irish parliamentarians warn us that the commemoration of the 50th anniversary of the Rising 'contributed to the environment from which the troubles emerged later'.[2] So now we know why the 30-year conflict in the north of Ireland broke out – the 50th anniversary commemorations of the Easter Rising whipped republicans up into such a frenzy that they thought 'let's start killing people'. These overwrought warnings touch on an almost paranoid fear of ordinary people engaging in spontaneous mass celebration of this key event in Irish history. Republicans marching to commemorate 1916 did not cause the troubles. They were caused by sectarianism built into the fabric of the six-county state. It was the denial of civil rights and the beating down of protests asking for civil rights that caused the emergence of the conflict – not the 1916 commemorations.

Part of the reason why the centenary is so sensitive is because of the legacy of conflict in the Six Counties and the current peace process.

Many politicians, writers and academics who support the peace process both fear the Centenary Celebrations and also see them as an opportunity. In effect, the Easter Rising is being used as a vehicle to promote and connect people to the peace process under the guise of reconciliation and respecting traditions. Hence, the signing of the Ulster Covenant, the First World War, the Easter Rising and other events are being collapsed together in what is now referred to as 'a decade of centenaries' and packaged as a means of promoting respect and mutual understanding between unionist and nationalists when it comes to remembering those who fought for Britain in the Great War and those who rose up against Britain in the Easter Rising.

Writers, politicians and other academics tell us that this decade of centenaries should be used to promote peace and reconciliation. In other words, we have the discipline of history being manipulated to suit a contemporary political imperative. In short, history is to be bastardised when it suits, in order to underpin the politics of the peace process. This is a dangerous and foolhardy approach.

An equally disturbing trend has been the attempt to silence and suppress those who wish to make a moral distinction between those Irish men who fought for the British army in World War One and those Irish republicans who fought against the British Empire in the Easter Rising. There is a moral equivalence, we are told. President Higgins, The Taoiseach, Enda Kenny, the majority of the media and writers warn against making a moral distinction. To challenge the orthodoxy of moral equivalence is to be divisive and irresponsible, they inform us.

But, to suspend critical judgement on the rights and wrongs of this historical period is to lose oneself in non-judgementalism and relativism. Let us make our position very clear at the outset. Those Irishmen who fought for the British Empire in the Great War fought for the wrong country and died for the wrong cause. Those Irish republicans who fought and died in the GPO and elsewhere fought for freedom and self-determination and against British colonialism – they fought for the right country and they died for a noble cause. The moral distinction between

5

these two groups is quite clear. We should not be afraid to tell the truth when looking back on those historical moments at the GPO and Somme, where Irishmen fought, killed and died.

The British-Irish Parliamentary Assembly Report expresses a fear that some people 'opposed to the progress made under the peace process in recent years, may attempt to exploit the anniversaries to project a negative message and further division between the communities in northern Ireland'. This reads as a coded warning to anyone who is not prepared to massage the history and politics of 1916 for feel-good purposes of the present. The second problem is that the Irish Parliamentary Assembly Report does just that. It contrives an ahistorical, manipulated and retrospective consensus about the legacy of 1916 and other events in order to bolster, in the crudest of ways, the contemporary peace process.

It is worth remembering the words of historian Roy Foster at this point, when he said that 'for all the well-meaning government rhetoric about "our shared history", revolutions are about antagonism, not reconciliation'. This is all the more true when it comes to the causes of the Easter Rising. No amount of fuzzy peace process language about shared pasts and futures can avoid the reality. The cause was hatred of British occupation of Ireland and a desire to challenge the barbarism of World War One. The Rising was about hatred of British colonialism, a willingness to deploy political violence and a willingness to die for a cause. Not much ambiguity there. As Thomas MacDonagh, one of the leaders of the Rising, wrote in a letter to his wife Muriel a few hours before his execution, 'I counted the cost of this and I'm ready to pay for it'. Joseph Plunkett, another of the executed leaders, was equally forthright as to what the Easter Rising was all about. In a letter to his fiancée Grace on the morning of his surrender, he wrote 'the Empire is dead: Ireland's journey to freedom continues'.

There is nothing wrong with historical revisionism in the

correct sense of the word. It is no bad thing to re-examine the past and try to understand its connection to where we are now. In this respect, we welcome the competing interpretations of the 1916 Rising that vie for people's attention. In fact, this book is a humble attempt to put on record our own interpretation of why the Rising happened and what its impact was in terms of legacy. Looking back through the historical records, what is striking is the extent to which the impact of the event was felt not only in Ireland and Britain, but right across the world. We argue that the international shockwaves and their effect on anti-First World War movements and politics mean that the 1916 Easter Rising was a historic event in global terms.

In chapter one, 'History wars', we examine the competing interpretations of the Easter Rising by re-visiting key anniversaries in previous decades. What shines through is the attempt by various groups to not only pass judgement on the men and women of 1916, but to take control and ownership of anniversary commemorations, as a way of trying to shut others out. This leads us to an assessment of historical revisionism and the battle of ideas waged between different historians and commentators in interpreting the legacy of Easter 1916.

Chapter two, 'The Rising in history', locates the Easter Rising in the wider context of inter-imperialist rivalries, which developed in the lead up to the Great War. One of the biggest mistakes people make when looking at the Rising is trying to understand it within the narrow context of Irish politics and history alone. Here, we deliberately contextualise the origins of the Rising emerging in response and as a challenge to the catastrophe of the First World War. Consequently, we draw out the links between inter-imperialist tensions, labour unrest in Britain and Ireland, and the growing revolt against the World War in both countries. The parades and beating drums, the flags and the arms shipments and the fighting of Easter 1916 would hardly have been possible in a different time. Putting the history of the Rising back into the story of the Great War we think greatly helps to explain a lot of what was really going on.

Chapter three, 'A shot that echoed around the world', examines reactions to the Easter Rising in Britain, Europe and the wider world. This section represents one of the central aims of the book, where we document the response of people across the globe to what was a world historic event. We reveal the shock of the British establishment, but also the admiration and support for the Rising, from a range of radical thinkers, activists and working-class people in Britain, from Sylvia Pankhurst to John MacLean. The Easter Rising was a bolt of lightning that inspired anti-imperialists from across the world to rise up against their colonial masters, and in this sense, its significance needs to be understood as stretching far beyond Europe. In this chapter, we document how Bolshevik leader Vladimir Lenin clearly grasped that the Rising was in fact the first anti-war uprising against the barbarism of the Somme. To those who try to label the Easter Rising a parochial squabble and sideshow to the Great War, this chapter will destroy such illusions. It reveals just how inspired progressive people were by the Easter Rising and the War of Independence from India to Burma, and from Trotsky to Ho Chi Minh.

Chapter four, 'Revising the Rising', analyses the attempts by various historians to evaluate the motivations and historical impact of Easter 1916. Some historians accuse Connolly and Pearse of promoting sectarianism and creating partition. After examining the various debates between different groups, we identify where the revisionists had a point, and where they did not. Our argument here is that at heart, the real contest in Irish history writing is not between old fashioned, nationalist, mainstream historians and bold, daring revisionists on the other side. Rather, we conclude that some historians, in keeping with the outlook of much of the Irish intelligentsia throughout the 20th century, recoil from Irish nationalism and republicanism because it is popular. We draw out how some are motivated more by fear of grass roots republicanism than by academic rigour.

Chapter five, 'Historical Memory and the Peace Process', looks at the politics of commemoration, and the way that the official Decade of Centenaries has been framed to downgrade the Rising by drowning the event in a whole host of other commemorations – of the Battle of the Somme, the Dublin lock-out and even the signing of the Ulster Covenant. Here we take issue with the idea that all those who suffer should be honoured, and argue instead that some causes are more honourable than others.

Thanks are due to Kevin Bean, Phil Ferguson, Eve Kay, Kirk Leech and Michael Silvestri, and also to Michael Fitzpatrick, Phil Mullan, Frank Furedi and Aidan Campbell for their work on Ireland and the national question over the years.

We dedicate the book to the memory of Leo Gabriel O'Neill, republican and socialist.

Chapter one

History wars

Who's afraid of the Easter Rising? 100 years ago, on Easter Monday 1916, a few hundred men started a rebellion against British rule in Ireland. They seized the General Post Office in Dublin where they read out a proclamation inaugurating the Irish Republic. Though they fought bravely their forces were divided before the Rising began. After a week of intense artillery bombardment the Rising was crushed, the rebels rounded up and their leaders executed.

Within three years the Irish people had turned their back on the British Empire and elected a rebel parliament. What looked to many at the time like a quixotic act turned out to be the 'blood sacrifice' that would set Ireland on the road to freedom.

The Rising of 1916 was celebrated on the 50th anniversary in 1966 as the foundational act of the Irish Republic. A film was made, medals were struck, and the act was celebrated across the land. 25 years later on the 75th anniversary, in 1991, the Taoiseach Charlie Haughey rushed through a 'short, dignified ceremony' and issued some stamps commemorating the Rising. The whole event was over so quickly that some of the officials taking part were locked out of the Post Office.

The commemoration of historical events can be important affairs for states; the ownership of the past establishes the hierarchy in the present. Telling a national story is a way of building solidarity. But the origins of the Irish state of today in the Rising of 1916, and the independence struggle that followed it, have proved deeply uncomfortable to its present-day leaders.

Between the anniversaries of 1966 and 1991 people's idea of the Rising had changed. Heroic sacrifice it seemed on the 50th anniversary, but 25 years later a lot of people were saying that it was the act of political extremists – even Fascists – that put the gun into Irish politics, at a terrible cost in human lives over the decades.

Between 1966 and 1991 all changed when guerrilla war broke out once again in the six north-eastern counties of the Province of Ulster – that part of Ireland that had not joined the Free State in 1921, but instead had been kept in the United Kingdom. The so-called 'troubles' broke out in 1969, a conflict first between Civil Rights protestors and the Northern Irish State, quickly overcome by a state of war between Irish republicans and the British Army; that war led many to despair that Irish republicanism would always tend towards violence.

Many remembered that the young men and women who took up the gun had often been moved by the 1966 celebrations commemorating the Easter Rising 50 years earlier. Innocent and cheerful celebrations, but did they inspire a new generation to take up arms in the cause of the Irish Republic?

Some of those who took part in the first civil rights protests in the Six Counties in 1969–70 wondered where the bright future of those days had gone. The mood of sixties protest gave way to sour warfare and even sectarianism. Does Ireland suffer under the burden of too much history, they worried?

Genuflecting to the totems of the Easter Rising was less liberation than conformism, they thought, the past weighing down upon the future. Historians and political scientists set about re-examining the history, bravely tearing down the heroes of yesteryear in books and articles. An oedipal revolt against the men of Easter began.

Truth to tell there was always a strong streak of distaste for the Easter Rising. Most obviously the British statesmen, military leaders and British propagandists and historians have painted a harsh picture of the Rising and the traditions it gave rise to – which is hardly surprising since the rebellion was made against them. In the Six Counties, the political leaders of the Northern

Irish State and the Orange Order that sustained them carried a special hatred for the men and women who challenged British rule in Ireland. In the south of Ireland, too, the respectable people who only wanted to hold together an orderly state and make their peace with the British Empire were shamed by that constant reprimand that the Easter Rising was to them: why is Ireland still divided?

Looking back at the history of Ireland in the 20th century many have properly focussed their attention on what is specific and unique to the country and its traditions. But looking today, in this parade of centenary commemorations, it is hard not to be struck by just how much the story of Ireland's uprising was a part and parcel of a conflict that was taking place across the whole world, the Great War, the First World War, from 1914 to 1919.

'The Easter Rising damaged the Irish psyche', said the former Taoiseach, John Bruton at a debate at the Irish Embassy on the centenary of the Irish Home Rule Bill, 1 July 2014. The Rising was 'completely unnecessary', and 'led directly to the brutal violence of the war of independence and the civil war that followed'. The Rising's leader Patrick Pearse 'had justified the provos' – the Provisional IRA.

These words are striking because the Easter Rising, the rebellion of 1916 led by Patrick Pearse, has until recently been held to be the beginning of Ireland's emergence as an independent state, with a government chosen by its own people – the very government that John Bruton led.

In Ireland today the history of the independence movement that sustained the people for so long is being re-written.

With the 100th anniversary of the rising approaching the *Irish Times* was genuinely worried. 'The Rising was a complex event', they wrote: 'There is a danger that shorn of context, it can be presented as a glorification of the cult of violence, as happened in 1966'.[1] The spectre of the 50th anniversary of the Rising, in 1966, is almost as problematic as the original event of 1916. That is because many believe that the forthright celebration of that anniversary led directly to the outbreak of conflict in the still-occupied Six Counties of northern Ireland in 1969. So, for example, a special report by the British-Irish Parliamentary Assembly worries that Eamon De Valera's celebrations in 1966 'may have contributed to the environment from which the troubles may have emerged later in the decade'. Celebrating history in Ireland, it seems, is fraught with fears of stirring up ancient hatreds.

Éamon de Valera inspecting the troops, Easter 1966

The Rising, claims the leading political commentator Stephen Collins, was a violent conspiracy that was out of keeping with the Irish Parliamentary Party of John Redmond. 'Most of our modern political leaders have far more in common with the values of the old Irish Parliamentary Party and its leader than they have with those who directed the activities of the Irish Republican Brotherhood' – the militants of the Rising. 'Yet our current generation of politicians', writes Collins, are 'falling over themselves to pay obeisance to revolutionary leaders whose values they don't actually share'. Angered by the revolutionary moment embedded in Irish politics, Collins protests that 'the majority of law-abiding people who live by democratic standards are required to despise those earlier generations who adhered to the same values' – Redmond and the Parliamentarians, he means – 'while honouring those who rejected them', the rebels.[2]

This view of the Rebels of 1916 would surely have been welcomed by English Tories of 100 years ago, but it is a surprise to hear an Irish political journalist dismiss the event that won Ireland its own parliament and right to debate its freedom as anti-democratic. Such, though, is the discomfort of the Irish political class with their own history, a discomfort that is driving them to dismiss it.

'I think 1916 is very problematic and the legacy is particularly problematic – the legacy of 1916 in the Republic', said Eoghan Harris, the television journalist and political commentator. Harris turned away from his republicanism of earlier days to compare the 1916 Easter Rising with the Loyalist-inspired promise of the Ulster loyalists to break Home Rule: 'I regard the Ulster Covenant of 1912 as a fundamentally delinquent political act, like I regard the 1916 Rising as a delinquent political act'.

The Easter Rising, Harris was saying, was 'what I call a delusionary reaction'. Pearse's view that 'if the Ulstermen have guns in their hands, we should have guns in our hands', was 'bullshit'. Sir Edward Carson, the Tory leader of the Ulster Covenanters, 'was very like Pearse in the kind of delusionary rhetoric he engaged in'. Harris, who had after all been a leading figure in Sinn Fein once, said he was 'very sorry that Pearse took up that kind of republicanism, which was delusionary and abstract compared to Wolfe Tone's republicanism'. According to Harris, Pearse was 'in a big tradition of European romanticism at that time, like a whole kind of fevered delusionary nationalism' ('to think that he could take German aid and there'd be no consequence to it').[3]

The commemoration of the centenary of the Easter Rising is all the more problematic because it falls in the middle of another centenary: that of the Great War. Eoghan Harris contrasts the illegitimate Ulster Covenant with the 'completely different' Battle of the Somme. Remembering the Great War is itself a difficult and painful business for nations that have struggled over the intervening decades to put the violent chauvinism that drove them to slaughter one another behind them. Juggling the competing demands of honouring the war dead and preserving the peace is a problem across Europe. With the events of 1916 it is all the more difficult because the nation itself came to independence through the struggles of that time.

In October 2012 the British-Irish Parliamentary Assembly drafted a special report called 'A Decade of Commemorations'. There the modern-day allies looked back nervously on their contested history. Hopefully, they argued that the 'British and Irish should commemorate histories together' – meaning the histories of the Great War and of the Easter Rising. Setting out their priorities they said that 'firstly we want to prevent the distortion of history that could be used to serve certain negative political movements'. Was this perhaps a slight at the British Education Minister, Michael Gove, who had deplored the pacifistic teaching of the British war effort? No. The fear was not one of British nationalism. Rather it was a fear of militant Irish republicanism. History, it seems, is too politically sensitive to be left to the historians, or to be allowed to speak for itself, but must be bent to meet the needs of today's elite. The 'Parliamentarians' set out their hope that the centenary should be used to 'work towards reconciliation'.

One way in which the Irish people are being asked to re-write their own history is to celebrate the militarism of the British Army in 1914. Though the meaning of the Easter Rising was a revolt against the beating of the Imperial Drum, Irish President Michael Higgins said at the dedication of a cross of sacrifice at Glasnevin Cemetery in Dublin, 1 August 2014, that 'we need to undo the disrespect that was sometimes shown to those who fought' in the 1914–19 war. Of course it would be truer to say that the disrespect was aimed at the recruiting sergeants who led those men to their slaughter. Still Higgins warmed to his theme of praising the sacrifices of British militarism: 'To all of the fallen in their silence we offer our own silence, without judgment, and with respect for their ideals as they knew them, and for the humanity they expressed towards each other'.

It was a painful formulation. What was the humanity that the armies of Britain, France and Germany expressed towards each other? Higgins' hope though was set out clearly enough. He wanted to avoid the judgment of the events of 100 years ago, and above all to silence those who stand in the tradition of the Easter Rising. It was a demand that the two competing goals of the conquest of Ireland by British Imperialism and the Irish people's revolt against militarism be put on an equal footing, smothered in a fog of silent sobbing.

Journalist Niall O'Dowd understood the true meaning of what the politicians and the elite were asking for: 'The glorifying of World War I and the denying of Easter 1916'. The historian Brian Hanley noticed that this newfound affection for honouring the war dead of the Great War comes from those who are critics of Irish republicanism.[4] The anniversary of the Rising has been celebrated before – every year, but more dramatically on the 50th (1966), 60th (1976) and 75th (1991) anniversaries. Each anniversary became a measure of the Irish people, and the establishment's attitudes towards their own history, and to the state they governed. The memory of the Rising grew in importance in the first 50 years, but it became more and more tendentious after 1966.

1991: The 75th anniversary of the Rising

1991 was the 75th Anniversary, and a very strange one it was. In the run-up to the event, the Irish Association met in Dublin to hear a talk given by Joseph Lee, a History Professor at Cork

University. 'The Commemoration of the Rising has become an embarrassment for many people because of the IRA campaign in northern Ireland', but also 'because the Ireland of the 1990s has failed to live up to the ideals of those who fought for an independent state'.

Like many historians, Lee was a little perplexed at the trouble his calling made, and wondered whether everyone should not calm down a bit. 'I think we should have more confidence in ourselves as a reasonable, normal people, who do not have a tradition of bloody hands to any greater extent than any other people.' Looking back at the newspapers that were being published in 1916 he was perplexed by:

> their treatment of the war in Europe in which vast numbers were being slaughtered in one of the most stupid of all wars, and hear their rolls of honour, their tributes to gallantry and so on, for the poor devils getting slaughtered in France, and then there is the revulsion against the Rising.

Even back in 1991, when the peace process that ended the shooting war in northern Ireland was only in preparation, the Irish Association had asked the Ulster Unionist Party leader David Trimble to give his views on the commemoration. Trimble was looking for as much common ground as he could find, but he was not about to dissolve the Unionist position. There was, he said, 'ambiguity' in Ireland about the Rising because whatever the links are between the Provisional IRA and 1916, 'they are the heirs of the mythology of 1916'. Celebrating founding myths was quite natural, thought Trimble, and 'something with which Unionists were very familiar'. The republican 'myths' it seemed were of a different order to those legitimate ones, because of what they said for the present. Trimble was troubled:

> Your problem here, if I may say so, in the Irish Republic, is

that the myths surrounding 1916 are not easily confined to the present State and, *of course*, are *meaningless* if they try to extend beyond it.[5]

Trimble took heart from the difficulties that the Irish in the south were having over how to commemorate their founding myth. The 'confused and ambivalent response' of southern politicians to the 75th anniversary meant that it would not impinge on Protestants in the north. That was a lot better than the 'tub-thumping of 1966', the 50th anniversary, whose more thoroughgoing commemoration upset Protestants. According to the Ulster Unionist Party MP 'the 1966 fiftieth anniversary celebrations in the North were a significant factor in starting the current troubles'. Just when the administration in the six north-eastern counties of Ulster was 'ushering in a new era of accommodation, the old republican ghosts started walking and the Northern nationalists walked after them'.

Of course many will remember that it was the other way around. The Irish Republican Army was nowhere to be seen in the Six Counties when the Civil Rights demonstrations first started asking for equality. Only *after* the Protestant Regime in Stormont Castle sent its B-Special police force in to batter the protestors, and then *after that* when loyalist paramilitaries started attacking Catholic neighbourhoods in the lea of the 12th of July Celebrations, did anyone moot the idea of a self-defence force, let alone the re-born IRA.

But in 1991 Trimble was hoping for more than ambiguity, and that the 'interesting thinking' of the revisionist historians would percolate through to wider society in the south. Trimble's more reflective view is that 'they could have had for the asking what they got in 1922 – and without the bloodshed and the legacy of that bloodshed' – or in other words, Britain would have granted the south a Free State even if there had been no Rising in Easter 1916. More bluntly, Sammy Wilson of the populist Democratic

Unionist Party, said that the general Protestant population just does not care that much about Irish history, except 'to recall that while both Protestant and Catholic Irish were out fighting in France, they were being stabbed in the back here at home'. Chris McGimpsey of the Ulster Unionist Party was less interested in the subtleties of historical revision, saying plainly that 'most northern Protestants would regard most people who celebrated the Easter Rising as sneaking regarders of today's Republican terrorists':

> People here will be looking very carefully at the way the Irish Government commemorates it. If a Fianna Fail Government plays it down, Northern Protestants will take it as a signal that the Southern state is less comfortable about its violent republican origins than would have been the case with previous generations. They would welcome that.[6]

Since the Six Counties in Ulster were withheld from an independent Ireland, and the Protestant minority on the island made the custodians of British rule there, it is to be expected that their leaders would disdain the Rising of 1916. Perhaps less predictable was the hostility of so many of Ireland's own intellectuals for the commemoration.

Queen's University's Paul Bew, debating with an old comrade from Sinn Fein, the Workers' Party, thought 'the spirit of 1916 cannot be reclaimed' – it was simply redundant: 'the Era opened up by the Easter Rising has come to an end', and he warned Tomas MicGiolla that 'attempts to reclaim its spirit by fringe nationalist groups are futile'. Wrongheaded, too, he thought, was the claim that the Irish revolution had never been properly consummated. On the contrary 'in so far as it could be it was made the guide to government policy for forty years and it failed'.[7]

The political commentator Fintan O'Toole looking back at the

1916 Rising saw it as just more of the same bloodshed that had engulfed the rest of the world in the years 1914–1919: 'a minor footnote to the First World War, which is itself one of the great idiocies of human history'. 'The 2000 members of the IRB are an eccentric subdivision of the 200,000 people who fought in the First World War', he wrote. O'Toole was so distanced from the events of the First World War that he could not tell the difference between those who were promoting it, and those who were rebelling against it.[8]

In 1991 journalist Kevin Myers was reporting 'yet another example of the triumph of revisionist historians, who regard the 1916 Rising as a deeply undemocratic conspiracy which cast as much darkness across Irish history as it did light'. Myers thought it 'indisputable that the Rising was a profoundly undemocratic event, the essence of which was the unmandated killing of people in the streets of Dublin'. Myers went further than David Trimble's view that the Irish would have got a free state in 1922 if there had been no Rising, saying 'Ireland in 1916 was a constitutional democracy which had already been granted Home Rule, to be enacted when the war was over'. Moreover, thought Myers, the peace conference at Versailles and the League of Nations being very sympathetic to the creation of smaller states would have been amenable to Irish claims.

Quite which Irish nation it would have been appealing to the League of Nations in 1919 for their own Free State is not easy to imagine. The moderate Nationalist Party leaders that had brought Ireland into the bloodbath of the Great War had won the sacrifice of Irish lives, but only under English officers, and without even a flag or badge to say they were Irish. Participation in the slaughter did not rally the nation around the Nationalist Party, but instead around those who had campaigned against conscription and the war, Sinn Fein. Ireland was not a constitutional democracy, but a military dictatorship under a Lord Lieutenant and the sweeping provisions of the Defence of the

Realm Act.

According to historian Robert Owen Dudley Edwards, 'the measures of self-government in 1920 and 1921 cannot be said to have been the inevitable consequence of the 1914 Act'. 'Home Rule', he wrote in 1966, 'had been obliged to give way in 1914 and again in 1916 and 1918'. Moreover 'Unionism after the 1919 peace might have proved even more intimidating but for the new spirit in Ireland since 1916'. Historian Nicholas Mansergh went so far as to say 'force, of the threat of it, delivered the goods, where constitutionalism, after long trial, had not.'[9]

In 1991, the nay-sayers had the *Irish Times* editorial writer on their side. On 29 March they published:

The Easter Rising was a calculated conspiracy to spill blood. Those who planned it knew that most of it would be that of innocent uninvolved people – as was the case. It was profoundly undemocratic. Its object was to sweep away moderation and compromise.

It is hard to imagine any other country so convinced that its own origins were mistaken. Britons seem quite relaxed about the fact that their country's independence, its breakaway from the domination of the Pope in Rome, was undertaken to get King Henry VIII a divorce, and that it led to the sacking of the monasteries and mass persecution of Catholics.

The Rising was not just violent and undemocratic, said the *Irish Times*,

it is possibly true that without the Easter Rising an independent Irish State would have come into existence anyway. It is also possible to argue that if there had been no recourse to arms, Ireland today would not have been divided and the North would be at peace.

Imagine if the *Washington Post* carried an editorial saying that America would probably have been better off if there had been no War of Independence. Ireland's doubts about the Rising speak to a profound lack of self-respect.

On 9 March the paper's Parliamentary correspondent Joe Carroll reported that 'for the beleaguered Taoiseach, 1991 has opened a Pandora's box of anniversaries to challenge Fianna Fail's claim to be the true republican party'.

Not all intellectuals were so hard on the women and men who went out in Easter 1916. Writer John McGahern wondered that 'the signatories of the Proclamation were poor writers and intellectuals' – 'a more unlikely crowd to spark a nation would be hard to imagine'. McGahern took a different view, too, of the relation of the modern nation to the Rising. 'The spirit of the Proclamation was subverted in the Free State that grew out of that original act of self-assertion in the General Post Office'. Jarring with the often-claimed triumphalism of past commemorations, McGahern remembered, 'the 1916 Rising was not considered to be of any great importance in the country I grew up in':

> In fact it was felt secretly to have been a mistake. "What was it all for?" was a puzzlement as widespread as the Rosary.
>
> Certainly it meant little to the people in the crowded boat trains, the men who worked on the roads or had a few acres and followed de Valera's dream, to the men and women who waited until they were too old to marry.

There was, he felt 'a deep ambivalence to the whole arrangement that was called a country'. Tomas MacGiolla also had memories of the way the story was told in his youth: that it was a pointless, if beautiful, gesture. He 'was taught that Easter Week was a Poet's Rebellion of idealists, a blood sacrifice inspired by the crucifixion of Christ, futile, but brave and heroic'. McGahern and MacGiolla both wanted to save what they thought the true meaning of the Proclamation was.

'I think we can best honour 1916 by restoring those rights and freedoms which were whittled away from the nation as a whole in favour of the dominant religion', said McGahern: 'We should put the spirit of the Proclamation into our laws'. MacGiolla fixed on James Connolly and recalled 'he was fighting for socialism, for independence, for neutrality and against war'.[10]

Republicans, including Gerry Adams and Bernadette McAliskey put pressure on the government with a 'Reclaim the Spirit of 1916' committee. On the other side, Fine Gael put pressure on the government to 'ensure that this year's 1916 ceremonies include all the Irishmen who died fighting in France that year, and to disown the violent campaign of the Provisionals in the North'. When Fianna Fail chief whip Bertie Ahern proposed a restricted programme, he was accused by Captain James Kelly of 'giving expression to the cult of revisionism'. Even the Taoiseach's special adviser Martin Mansergh took issue:

> The liberal intelligentsia North and South are much attracted to the notion that 1916 and the subsequent development of the Irish State on Gaelic and Catholic lines steadily widened divisions. Some have even made the absurd and far-fetched claim that it was republicanism that partitioned Ireland.

The minister Desmond O'Malley, on the other hand, said 'it was understandable that people of goodwill of all political persuasions should shy away from any drum-beating or flag-waving about 1916, lest it offer any comfort or misguided endorsement to today's IRA murder campaign'.[11]

Fintan O'Toole redirected his own tortured assessment of the 1916 Rising into an imaginative resolution, that the consummation of the Proclamation is in the Treaties of the European Union:

1991 is not just the 75th Anniversary of the Rising, it is also the year before 1992. Whatever its rights and wrongs, 1916 started something in blood and banners and glorious symbols which we are just about to end in ECUs and exchange rate mechanisms and the free flow of goods. They may not have known it but what the men and women of 1916 fought for was an Irish seat at the European Table. The Rising began with a European conflict and it may well end at long last, with a European integration.[12]

Time has not been kind to this idea, but you can see how it made some sense in 1991. The claim that the European Union was a resolution of intra-European conflict has been very valuable to the leaders of the member states, and it seemed to fit Ireland very well. Since then, though, one of the most pro-European nations, Ireland, has been wracked by anti-European protests. Irish voters rejected by referendum the Treaty of Nice to enlarge the Union in June 2001; embarrassed and angry, the political class made the electorate vote again the following year, and with some arm-twisting got a majority vote. Then, again, the Irish voters rejected the Treaty of Lisbon, entrenching European governing structures, in 2007, only to be made to run the election a second time, in 2009, when they finally agreed. The anti-EU coalitions have rallied minority parties, including Sinn Fein and the Greens, outside the mainstream in a revolt against the political system. Their background is a biting reversal of the economic boom Ireland enjoyed under the European Union's years of low interest rates, and the imposition of harsh fiscal limits on public spending. If anyone today was to make the link between the struggles over sovereignty in the 20th century and the issue of Europe it would more likely be to equate the loss of sovereignty under the British Empire and the Union.

Given the soul-searching on the part of the chattering classes it was not going to be easy to organise the actual ceremony on the day. The *Irish Times* had already warned the Government against the 'dangerous simplicities which sponsored the 1966 celebrations'. So it was in the Dáil that the Taoiseach Charles Haughey promised a short and dignified ceremony with no trimmings. As the official notice said:

To mark the 75th Anniversary of the 1916 Rising, a Military Ceremonial will be held on Easter Sunday ... at the General Post Office.

This will be a short and dignified ceremony involving the reading of the proclamation and hoisting the National Flag.

The President and the Taoiseach will attend.

Even then the opposition Fine Gael front bench decided they would not grace even as guarded an expression of national sentiment as this.

Reporter Joe Carrol told the story: 'The Easter Week rebels held out for a week in the GPO but it only took fifteen minutes to commemorate the Rising 75 years later.'

The whole event was not truly public at all. The small handful of veterans of 1916 were not invited, until the Taoiseach pointed out that this was a mistake. The only lasting commemoration was a set of stamps issued, and an information video about the rising. Some of the guests of An Post who were not quick enough on their feet and fell behind the official party 'found the doors of the GPO firmly shut'.[13] The event was more than short; it was hasty, and shifty, not dignified. Whether the Ulster Unionists Chris McGimpsey and David Trimble were satisfied that the Rising Commemoration had been shame-faced enough is not known, but in the eyes of the world, Dublin made it clear that Ireland was far from being at peace with itself.

So who are these historical revisionists?

Among the nervous reactions to 1916 a school of Irish revisionist historians are often mentioned. In recent times that would have meant Paul Bew, Austen Morgan and Henry Patterson. They have made a name for challenging the alleged nationalist bias of mainstream history, and have worked to clear away the myths of national resurrection, including those they see in histories of the Easter Rising.

All three were born in northern Ireland around 1950, and have been academics, notably at Queen's University, Belfast and the University of Ulster. Austen Morgan wrote a history of the Belfast working class in the early century, a biography of James Connolly and other books and chapters, though today he works as a lawyer in London. Paul Bew and Henry Patterson wrote books about the modernisation of Ireland and also about the loyalist of northern Ireland. Patterson is Professor of Politics at the University of Ulster, and Paul Bew is Professor of Politics at Queen's.

This generation of 'historical revisionists' were all on the left of northern Irish politics, supporters of the Northern Ireland Civil Rights Association, and all associated with the left-wing republican 'Sinn Fein', from which the Provisional IRA split off to take up arms against Britain in 1969. Many of the themes they took up are developments of the arguments made by official Sinn Fein against the more militant, and supposedly romantic, nationalists of the Provisional IRA. Since 1969 their trajectory has been towards mainstream Unionism and constitutional politics.

As much as the current school called 'historical revisionists' have added to the debate over nationhood, it would be fair to say that many of the themes they have developed had already been raised by an earlier generation that sought to reconsider the national history. Robert Dudley Edwards was Chair of Modern Irish History at University College Dublin from 1945 until his retirement. His children Ruth and Owen wrote biographies of Pearse, Connolly, and Parnell. They also collaborated with Conor Cruise O'Brien, who would do most to argue the case against militant Irish nationalism. This generation of southern critics of mainstream nationalism were mostly supporters of the Irish Labour Party, and O'Brien – who had been born into a staunch republican family – served as a Labour Minister in a coalition government led by the Fine Gael party's Liam Cosgrave from 1973-1977. Like the later, northern generation, O'Brien and the Dudley Edwardses sharpened up their polemics in a struggle against the revival of militant nationalism in the north, beginning in the seventies. An historian who stands between the two waves of 'historical revisionism' is Roy Foster, author of *Paddy and Mr Punch* and many other books.

'Historical Revisionists' is a clunky phrase that makes the argument sound like the split between the Maoists and the Khruschevites in the 1960s. Later we will go on to argue that it is a misnomer and that all history writing is in the nature of a revision of the understanding that went before. The spur to greater historical understanding is one happy by-product of what has been for too many people a very bitter and painful conflict. For all that, much of the history writing that has taken place has been too bent to serving political ends, whether laudatory or critical, which can frustrate the objectivity of the endeavour. In our treatment of the writers under question we are seeking to isolate the tendentious parts of the argument, and look at them, happy to welcome the many additions to the store of knowledge in all these books.

1966: The 50th anniversary of the Rising

A great deal has been made of the 1966 commemoration and its supposed contribution to the return of armed conflict in the north three years later. Reading some commentary it seems that the remembering of the Rising in 1966 is in danger of overshadowing the real Rising in 1916. With hindsight the official celebrations are not so out of keeping with the pageantry of the times. Most nations honour their war heroes and founding fathers, as the Americans did in the 200th anniversary of 1776, or the British did at Winston Churchill's funeral in 1965. In 1966, the Irish government organised a march of 600 veterans of the Easter Rising that was watched by 20,000. An essay-writing competition for school children added to the popular character of the event, as did a film of the events of 1916, Cuimhnicheán, broadcast on Radio Telefis Eireann.

As it is told in hindsight, the fervent national myth of 1916 relayed in 1966 had no room for the many Irishmen who fought in the British army. At the time, though, Taoiseach Sean Lemass gave a speech honouring the

tens of thousands of generous young Irishmen who, responding to the call of their Parliamentary leaders, had volunteered enthusiastically to fight, as they believed, for the liberty of Belgium.[14]

Though in retrospect many claim that the 1966 pageant invigorated militant Irish republicanism, at the time Sinn Fein were pointedly side-lined from the events by officials of the Irish state, and bitterly critical of their treatment. They held a separate rally, at Glasnevin Cemetery, and dismissed the official celebrations as propaganda for the state. In the Sinn Fein paper the *United Irishman* they wrote 'the squabbling over the bones of the 1916 martyrs has reached disgusting proportions', under the headline 'The Vultures Pounce'.

'It is fashionable now', they commented, 'to be party to the commemoration of the men of 1916 ... because the establishment has given its dubious blessing to the commemoration'. Father Patrick Malone wrote in to the paper to complain that the celebrations were premature 'because the ideals, principles and aspirations of the 1916 martyrs have not been carried through'.

The official events were called 'parades and processions galore', 'ballyhoo and celebrations', 'desperately patriotic', and the official spokesmen parodied: 'Well it's all over for another fifty years, but it was grand while it lasted'. The one striking republican protest in the south, the dynamiting of Nelson's pillar in Dublin was done by a breakaway group of left-wing republicans, led by Joe Christle, who had been expelled from the IRA years before, and Sinn Fein condemned the action at the time. In the north it was a different story. There the *United Irishman* reported a massive march starting at Casement Park, Belfast on 17 April 1966.[15]

A collection of essays on 1916 edited by Owen Dudley Edwards was published that year. A post-script was written by Conor Cruise O'Brien. It was a remarkable essay, thinking of his later journey. On the face of it O'Brien in 1966 sings the praises of the men and women of 1916. 'It is quite proper and fitting that Dublin should have held commemoration in 1966', he wrote, and even reflected 'on how the spirit of Easter 1916 may be at work in the wide world'. In those heady days of the 1960s O'Brien counts the Viet Cong, in their fight against US imperialism, as a part of the spirit of 1916 at work in 1966. O'Brien derives from the spirit of the Rising a mandate for rebellion. 'There was nothing official about the Easter Rising, from any point of view an entirely unauthorized undertaking', he wrote, adding, 'Connolly's writings speak not to governments but to men and women'.

O'Brien's claim to the spirit of 1916, though, was the platform for a sharp criticism of the supposed heirs to the Rising, the Irish State in 1966. 'The nation for which he [Pearse] died never came about', wrote O'Brien. Of the official celebrations he wrote 'in Dublin this year, were held the funeral ceremonies of the Republic proclaimed fifty years ago'. O'Brien is sharp on the mismatch between the hopes of the Rising and the reality of the Irish State, but also on the burden of historical memory and genuflection to the heroes of the past upon modernity and the young:

My generation grew into the chilling knowledge that we had failed, that our history had turned into rubbish, our past to a "trouble of fools" [Yeats]. With this feeling it is not surprising that the constant public praise for the ideals of Pearse and Connolly should have produced in us bafflement rather than enthusiasm. We were bred to be patriotic, only to find that there was nothing to be patriotic about; we were republicans of a republic that wasn't there.

O'Brien captures well the way that the revolutionary spirit of yesterday had been hi-jacked by the authoritarians of today. With a little embarrassment, O'Brien explains that it was once his job, as assistant to Sean MacBride, to help in the Irish government's campaign against partition, the separation of the six northern-most counties still governed by Britain from Ireland. The official campaign, he explains, was bogus, a 'cavernous inanity'. The object of the official anti-partition campaign 'was to console ourselves for the rubbish our history had turned into':

> We consoled ourselves by reiterating, to our own satisfaction, the classic arguments for a free and united Ireland and by demonstrating, likewise to our own satisfaction, the perfidy of our enemies.

He meant that the campaign was not meant to succeed in changing the fact of partition, but was instead addressed to a home audience, to make them think that the government was doing the right thing. O'Brien even contrasts the IRA's campaign against partition positively against the government campaign. 'All this pseudo-activity', he said of the official anti-partition campaign, 'had a practical and somewhat sinister function … It enabled the state to punish with a good conscience young men in the Irish Republican Army.' He goes on to contrast the IRA's 'raiding barracks in Ulster' with the government's 'sending bundles of booklets to Bootle', with the clear meaning that the former are real, and the latter tokenistic.[16] In their rhetorical form, at least, O'Brien's criticisms of the Irish Government celebrations were not that different from the *United Irishman*'s.

In 1972, as the Labour Party's spokesman on the north, O'Brien was sharply critical of republicanism proper, not token republicanism. In *States of Ireland*, part memoir, part historical essay, he was responding to the Ulster crisis, when the Northern Irish state opened fire upon civil rights protestors, provoking an all-out war between the IRA and the British Army. O'Brien was blunt that when he heard that the army had shot dead 13 civilians on 'Bloody Sunday' he was mostly concerned about the way that the issue would be taken up by militant republicans. The book was, remembered Austen Morgan, 'a profoundly moral deconstructing of the lies Irish nationalists tell themselves', while John Hume saw it as an apology for Unionism (a judgment that O'Brien bridled at, at the time, but then accepted in retrospect).

In *States of Ireland* O'Brien planted the myth that the commemorations of 1966 were responsible for the later conflict, since they 'encouraged a recrudescence of the IRA'. 'These celebrations had to include the reminder that the object for which the men of 1916 sacrificed their lives – a free and united Ireland – had still not been achieved', he wrote.

The general calls for rededication to the ideals of 1916 were bound to suggest to some young men and women, not only that these ideals were in practice being abandoned but that the way to return to them was through the method of 1916: violence applied by a determined minority.[17]

The view that the Dublin celebrations of 1966 were responsible for 'the recrudescence of the IRA' only helped to minimise the true cause, which was the O'Neill administration in the Six

Counties, its discrimination against Catholics and its violent response to the Civil Rights Association.

1976

O'Brien's attitude to the republicans hardened. Despite his big claims about democracy and liberalisation, as a minister in the government, he championed a bill that barred Sinn Fein from radio and television. The preparations for the 60th anniversary fell to the Fine Gael/Labour Coalition that he served. O'Brien's own views were set out in a talk he gave at the Ilkley Festival of Literature in 1975. There O'Brien claims to have uncovered a common failing of poets and politicians to think that they can achieve immortality 'through being remembered' for fantastic words or deeds. Politicians, he argues, are 'like other people in being the product not only of actual history, which is general unknowable and unknown, but also of "history" as it is general taught in their time and place, which in most times and places will be an inspirational myth designed to unify the nation and inspire it with a sense of pride in its past'. But politicians are different in that 'the inspirational version of history becomes abnormally important to them, so that they wish to enter into it, become part of it, and through it become immortal'.

The IRA, he claimed, gave this motive a 'particularly pure and deadly form', and 'one permanent feature of such a movement is the conception of history as a series of blood sacrifices enacted in every generation'. O'Brien recalls that the poet Yeats, who had woven a pretty national heroine in Cathleen ni Houlihan, worried on his deathbed 'Did that play of mine send out certain men the English shot?' O'Brien says, 'yes, it did'.

He goes further, asking 'what is the difference between the play Cathleen ni Houlihan and the Easter Rising of 1916?' And 'can we say flatly that one is fiction and the other real life?' O'Brien explains himself: 'If the participants in the real life action have taken in the fiction as a gospel or a sacrament that is a trans-

Did Maud Gonne MacBride bewitch Irishmen to fight, when she played Cathleen ni Houlihan in Yeats' play?

forming spiritual agency'. 'To minds that are possessed by that idea of sacrifice' there can be no appeal to rational sentiment. The objective is to become part of history, 'to achieve immortality by getting one's self killed for Ireland's sake'.[18]

The Minister for Posts and Telegraphs was getting carried away. Literary men are apt to think that literature has unimagined powers, and the poets are, as Shelley dreamed 'unacknowledged legislators for mankind'. For that matter farmers think that everything grows out of the ground, and engineers that everything is motion, pivots and momentum. Most of all O'Brien was just too snooty to try to understand the practical challenges that drove the nationalist population in the north to rebel against their conditions; and too selfish to understand that some people believe in causes that are larger than themselves, without thereby being prey to messianic delusions.

In the Thomas Davis Lecture, broadcast on Radio RTE, the historian Liam de Paor ('nationalist historian', O'Brien called him) said O'Brien's claim that 'this is essentially a literary question since history is a branch of literature was a solipsism' that 'denies the possibility of discerning objective historical truth'. In an aside de Paor claimed that O'Brien's 'own writings in recent years have shown a marked tendency to handle history in a distinctly literary way'. Against O'Brien's emphasis on the mythical de Paor took issue, saying 'history is no more unknowable and unknown than a great many other areas of human experience in spite of myths'.

De Paor took issue with 'the suggestion that our history took a wrong turning from the pursuit of political ends by parliamentary means to the pursuit of them by other means'. To de Paor that was to 'make the mistake of trying to direct history to suit present views or needs'. This could not be done, he said. 'The past was what happened, not the infinite possibilities of what might have happened.'[19]

Here de Paor was turning the revisionists' allegations against national history around and back on them. It was O'Brien who was dismissing objective history and making it into a tool for ideological purposes. It was a compelling defence of the objectivity of history, in the face of its politicisation, which, against expectation, he was throwing in the face of O'Brien and those who would today be called revisionists.

In another comment piece de Paor looked at 'The GPO tradition' and tried to clear away some of the clutter that had been heaped up around the question. Most importantly de Paor insisted on putting the Rising in the historical context of the Great War undertaken by the British Empire.

'The men who took the Post Office, it is often pointed out these days, acted without a popular mandate', wrote de Paor, 'but then there were very few of those to be had when the ordinary rules of civilised political procedure had been suspended in favour of the barbarism that was then going on in France and the Middle East'. De Paor explained that when 'war was exalted by the whole western world as the arbiter of nations' destinies and the means by which men might achieve and display the nobility in their natures', then 'the Volunteers took the rulers of their world, perhaps too literally, at their word, and derived their mandate from their own undoubted courage'. And once 'the end of the war made more normal politics possible again ... they won a retrospective support ... registered in popular votes'.

Against the stereotype, it was the 'nationalist' de Paor who was trying to stop the politicisation of history, while O'Brien was fighting against the mythical Cathleen ni Houlihan. De Paor hoped that it would become 'easier to treat the 1916 Rising for what it was, a matter of history, as it receded in time and the bewitching and bewildering glamour of myth faded'. To those who saw the emergency in the north as intimately related to 1916, de Paor had the wit to challenge 'has the 1916 rising a bearing on the present crisis? No.'[20]

Too late. O'Brien was bewitched – and bewildered. The Cabinet of which he was a member grappled with the question. De Paor had heard at the beginning of March 1976 that 'the Sixtieth anniversary will be treated publicly in a fairly perfunctory fashion' ('we live in a very different State from that which celebrate the fiftieth anniversary'). Then it became clear, as the *Guardian* newspaper was pleased to report that 'Dublin will not be formally celebrating the sixtieth anniversary of the 1916 Rising this Easter'. To the *Guardian*'s editors it seemed clear that 'credit for enticing more and more people away from the Provisionals must go to Dr Conor Cruise O'Brien', for his 'efforts to dig Republican mythology from under the Provisionals feet'. They were glad that 'statements by him on Ireland's recent history, which were considered outrageous five years ago, are more and more becoming the country's accepted wisdom'.[21]

But in the end the anniversary of the Rising would not be quiet, because the Cabinet, 'in an unexpected move', took the extraordinary step of putting a ban on its commemoration. The ban on Sinn Fein's planned march and rally 'is the first imposed on any demonstration in the Republic since the turbulent thirties'.[22] O'Brien and Taoiseach Cosgrave were to be found tilting at the windmills of 1916 after all. The *Guardian* might have hoped that O'Brien's was the received wisdom in the country, but they had mistaken the government for the country.

Provisional Sinn Fein held an illegal commemoration in 1976:
Irish Photo Archive

According to the *Irish Times* 'about ten thousand people attended a parade and meeting which had been banned by the Government'. The Dublin Government had downgraded and sought to deny Easter Week, 1916; Sinn Fein's Ruari O'Bradaigh said: 'We do not deny it, we uphold it, and we cherish it'. Daithi O'Conaill relished the government's tactical error in handing authority for the nation over to the republicans, saying that 'a group of people who claim to be a Government deplore Easter Week and all that it stands for'. He promised that 'the Republican movement would lead the people', and 'the time had come to challenge this shower in Dublin on every plane – political, economic and social'. 'Put your faith in the Provos and Ireland will be free', he said. It was child's play for Sinn Fein to cast the government as having banned the commemoration of the nation's founding on orders from Westminster. A government official could only protest that 'it's an embarrassment in the context of the North to have a Provo parade in the centre of the city'.[23]

Poet Michael O'Loughlin felt he had learned a lesson that year:

In an act of astonishing political opportunism, 1916 was revised. By 1976, and the 60th celebrations, a different tune was being played. For people of my generation, who were and who are, in an important sense, neither Republican nor non-Republican, this was a lesson they would never forget. To see history so swiftly rewritten was to realise that what was called history was in fact a façade behind which politicians manoeuvred for power.[24]

The Cosgrave government had made the Rising into a myth, and the republicans had taken it up to smack them over the head. When politicians, commentators and historians today repeat the claim that the 50th Easter Rising commemoration of 1966 blew up into a celebration of the Provos, they are misremembering. It was not the official government commemoration of 1966 that gave the IRA the platform, but the government ban on the commemoration in 1976.

Chapter two

The Rising in history

The Easter Rising took place in a time of war – the Great War of 1914–19 – which put great pressures on Ireland as it did the whole of Europe and much of the world. The 1914–19 war was a war between empires.

A world divided into empires

Between 1876 and 1914, the world's six biggest powers, Britain, France, Russia, Germany, Japan and America, had grabbed a territory two and a half times the size of Europe, and at the end of the period held enslaved over 500 million colonial people.[1] Paul Louis, in *Le Mercure de France*, April 1904, wrote that 'Imperialism is a general phenomenon of our age', and 'imperialism and socialism to a very large extent form the fundamental contradictions of our age'. Imperialism 'emerges everywhere as capitalism's supreme effort to preserve its wealth, political domination, social authority', and 'this involves territorial conquest, forcible or peaceful extension of possessions, closure of markets, creating of a closed empire'.

The British Empire in the first decades of the 20th century was greatly overextended, and in turmoil. In 1902 the British Empire had 50 colonies, covering a territory of 11,605,238 square miles, and subject peoples of 345 million. Its dominions included: Canada and the West Indies, first claimed in the 18th century; Australia; New Zealand; India; the East Asian states of Burma, Malaya that were all incorporated in the 19th century; and the African states of southern Africa and East Africa, the Sudan and – the 'veiled protectorate' – Egypt, which were claimed in the later 19th century. An official survey of 1910 admitted that forced labour was commonly used by the colonial authorities throughout the empire.

Ireland was not then counted a colony, but rather a nation within the United Kingdom, which it had been since the Act of Union of 1802, though settled and conquered earlier by the Tudors, Cromwell and the Dutch King William in 1689.

Having laid claim to global territories that extended as far as the combined empires of all other powers, the British Empire was struggling to maintain its control in the face of challenges from its rivals, and its own inner difficulties. Other European powers like France, Belgium, Germany and Italy emulated Britain's territorial reach, while the Russian Empire defended its great hinterland, and the Ottomans struggled to avoid collapse.

At the centre of this great expanse of plantations, farms, workshops and mines, was an industrial powerhouse built up in the cities of Birmingham, Manchester, Leeds, Newcastle, Glasgow and Belfast, commanded from the imperial capital, trading and banking centre, London. The crucible of the industrial revolution in 1815, and the workshop of the world by 1850, Britain was exhausted by the end of the 19th century, challenged by industrial rivals in the United States and a Germany unified under Bismarck.

Joseph Chamberlain's Tariff Reform League gained popular support for a policy of social imperialism, hiding British industry behind a protectionist wall between 1903 and 1914, though in the end the Government resisted.

Gearing up for the 'Second Industrial Revolution', with diesel and electric power displacing steam, light engineering alongside the stalwarts of steel and coal, chemicals and consumer goods strained economic growth. A long recession had dampened the economy in the later 19th century, but a return to prosperity also brought new demands from a revived labour movement led by more sophisticated workers. Two great waves of industrial unrest shook not just the British Empire but the whole world in 1905 and again in 1911–14.

The 'great unrest' in Britain saw strikes by miners, seamen, dockers, carters, tramway men, railway workers and even school children, and between 1911 and 1914 seventy million working days were lost through strike action. The upsurge was so shocking that the government went to war against its own people. In 1910 troops were used against rioters at the Rhondda Valley coal pits, with Hussars and Fusiliers invading the pit town of Tonypandy. Home Secretary Winston Churchill also sent a cavalry column into the East End to threaten striking dockers. Troops were called out against a rail strike in Chesterfield. In 1911 a general strike in Liverpool so terrified Home Secretary Churchill that he anchored a battleship off the port and fired upon strikers.

The 'great unrest' was at its greatest in Ireland in the Dublin lock-out of 1913, which we look at below.

The social turmoil was not only in the factories. Women, too, were on the march, fighting for the right to vote. The Women's Social and Political Union led by Emmeline and Christabel Pankhurst fought for the vote. The Suffragette campaign had snowballed, turning from constitutional lobbying to militant campaigns that included the burning churches and letterboxes, and smashing shop windows in the West End. The government answered with repression arresting women – many of whom went on hunger strike, and many of whom were force fed. On 18 November 1910 – 'black Friday' – Home Secretary told the police to make no arrests at a Suffragette demonstration outside parliament, but instead to beat the protestors into submission, which they tried to do in fighting that went on for five hours.

There was unrest in other countries, too, like the long and bitter Westmoreland miners' strike in the USA and the miners' strike in the Ruhr; and in 1909 a General Strike in Barcelona was called to protest against military conscription. These social conflicts stirred up violent reactionary forces: company goons and monarchist militias that added to the mood of disorder.

In the British Empire, too, there was unrest. Lord Curzon's plan to partition the old Province of Bengal stirred a protest that began with a boycott of British goods, and quickly spiralled into an underground campaign of bombs and assassinations. Activists Lajpat Rai and Bhal Gangadhar Tilak of Mahratta were deported; Bipin Chandra Pal, Chidambaran Pillai, Abdul Hasan Hasrat Mohani and many other activists were imprisoned in 1908.[2] In Egypt, in 1905, there was the Denashwai incident: it was triggered when English officers shot villagers' pigeons and wounded a local woman, provoking a riot that was later punished with summary executions. Shortly afterwards Mustafa Kamil founded the National Party, with the discrete support of Khedive Abbas Hilmi II. In London Madan Lal Dhingra was hung for the assassination of Sir William Curzon Wyllie in 1909.

The greatest blow against the British Empire would be struck in Dublin, in the Easter Rising.

The balance of power

Britain and the other Great Powers managed their relations to one another through the system of the 'balance of power'. Britain learned over the centuries to ally itself to different powers to prevent them from ganging up together to unite against her. The informal system of the 19th century had grown into an overwrought web of alliances and mutual defence pacts. The 'New Imperialism' of the 1890s had been an outlet for national rivalries, but the consolidation of their Empires meant that the European Powers were once again staring down each other, now over greatly extended borders across many continents.

In 1904 Britain and France agreed upon the 'Entente Cordiale'. It was an agreement to manage their long-standing rivalries, especially the rivalries between their Empires. 'In 1904, behind the innocuous terms of a diplomatic expression of friendship, the Entente Cordiale, were negotiated secret clauses by which France and Great Britain recognized each other's freedom of action respectively in Egypt and Morocco.'[3] Where Britain had brokered agreements with Germany in the 1890s, and tended to freeze out France, that changed as Germany began to be the bigger obstacle to Britain's position. In the Entente Cordiale Britain and France quietly agreed to divide up North Africa between them.

The Entente Cordiale froze out Germany, in particular frustrating her ambitions in Africa. As a counterweight to the Anglo-French accord, Germany sought to shore up its alliance with the Austro-Hungarian Empire, supporting Austria's claims in the Balkans. Among these were Austria's occupation of Bosnia-Herzegovina following the defeat of the Ottoman Empire in the war of 1879. In 1911 at Agadir, the German warship the Panther challenged France's authority in Morocco, in an incident that threatened conflict. Germany demanded compensation in cash or African territory at gunpoint. The socialist leader August Bebel saw the whole episode as 'in the first place an election manoeuvre'[4] and the British Chancellor David Lloyd George threatened that 'peace at that price would be a humiliation intolerable for a great country like ours to endure'.

Industrial competition translated directly into military competition in the naval contest. The rivalry over ship-building was the arms race of its day. The size of the rival powers' naval fleets was a sign of their industrial might turned into military reach and threatening to dominate world trade. Britain had had the monopoly over naval power throughout the 19th century. In 1898 Kaiser Wilhelm II set Admiral Tirpitz the task of challenging Britain's predominance. The German aim was to build their fleet up to two-thirds of the size of the British fleet. The standard was HMS Dreadnought, launched in 1906, so that all ships of that class became known as 'Dreadnoughts'. When the British saw what was happening, they committed themselves to massively increasing the size of their fleet to stop the Germans from catching up. Charles Dilke told Parliament on 22 March 1901, 'it is impossible to shut our eyes to the fact that there have been distinctly proposed to the German Houses, by Admiral Tirpitz, estimates which are based on the possibility of an outbreak of war with England'.

In the House of Commons on 29 March 1909 MP Arthur Lee moved a motion of censure against the government, claiming that 'the immediate provision of battleships of the newest type does not sufficiently secure the safety of the Empire'. 'The House and the country are perfectly right in the view that the situation is grave', said Sir Edward Grey, taking the criticisms in the motion. When the German shipbuilding plans were done, he said 'that fleet would be the most powerful which the world has ever yet seen'. At the same time, in the German deputies in the Reichstag demanded to know: 'Is Germany the armaments race leader?'

In 1912 Germany celebrated the centenary of the arms manufacturer Krupp, 'much as if it were a branch of the government, as in a sense it is', wrote the *Nation*. Head of the firm Gustav boasted:

Krupp cannon have thundered over the battlefields where German unity was fought for and won, and Krupp cannon are the energy of the German army and navy today.[5]

The arms race of the early 20th century was the cutting edge of the contest of empires. Inter-imperialist rivalry would tip over from a commercial struggle over markets into a contest of ships, guns and men.

National chauvinism v socialism

Britain's shipbuilding programme was not just aimed at Germany. It was aimed at the British public, who were called upon to champion the cause of naval supremacy. Chauvinistic campaigns calling for more Dreadnoughts gripped the imagination of the British middle classes, and the elite breathed a sigh of relief that militarism was proving a popular challenger to socialism.

The Dreadnought campaign was championed in Horatio Bottomley's patriotic journal *John Bull* (founded 1906), whose circulation reached half a million in 1910, and in 1912 Noel Pemberton Billing launched *The Imperialist: A journal devoted to the progress of the Empire and its people*, championing air power; in France Charles Maurras founded Action Française. As Bertrand Russell saw it, 'for the past ten years, under the fostering care of the Government and a portion of the Press, a hatred of Germany has been cultivated and a fear of the German Navy'. It was a campaign, he said that was 'fostered by the upper class as a distraction from social discontent'.[6]

One aspect of the growing militarisation of Europe in the 'imperialist epoch' was the great number of military and paramilitary parades. Patriotic military parades were the elite's alternative to the appeal of socialism, winning the people over from the red flag to the national one. Jack London wrote about the Coronation Day parade in 1902:

So it was along the whole line of march – force, overpowering force; myriads of men, splendid men, the pick of the people, whose sole function in life is blindly to obey, and blindly kill and destroy and stamp out life. And that they should be well fed, well clothed, and well-armed, and have ships to hurl them to the ends of the earth, the East end of London, and the 'East End' of all England, toils and rots and dies.[7]

In 1913 Kaiser Wilhelm ordered national celebrations for the centenary of Prussia's victory over Napoleon, just two years after the Agadir Incident had raised the temperature between the two countries.

As well as the official military parades there were unofficial paramilitary societies, too. German students joined duelling associations. The lifting of the siege of Mafeking in South Africa had led to a rash of patriotic demonstrations, with a great procession marching around the offices of the *Manchester Guardian* (which had been critical of the concentration camps) led by a band playing the death march from Saul. Baden Powell founded the Boy Scouts to train the next generation to meet such challenges. Action Française ran a youth wing, Les Camelots du Roi. The Polish Union of Active Struggle and the Rifleman's Association were founded to encourage rebellion against Russia. The Black Hundred group was founded to foment rebellion against Austrian rule in Bosnia. In Ireland, too, military parades would have a big impact.

There was a strong trend in elite opinion that wanted to see a suspension of democracy, that seemed to many to lead to far too much wrangling and politicking, deadlock and poor decisions (a mood that would reoccur in the 1930s, in the 1970s, and again in the first decade of the 21st century). In 1910 the British Chancellor David Lloyd George was fixated by the problems that faced the country. 'We were beset by an accumulation of grave issues – rapidly becoming graver', he wrote, and 'it was becoming evident to discerning eyes that the Party and Parliamentary System were unequal to coping with them'. Some of the problems he had in mind were 'the shadow of unemployment ... rising ominously on the horizon, our international rivals forging ahead at a great rate and jeopardising our hold on the markets of the world'. Worse, 'our working population, crushed into dingy streets with no assurance that they would not be deprived of their daily bread by ill-health or trade fluctuations, were becoming sullen and discontent'. Lloyd George also feared that 'Great nations were arming feverishly for an apprehended struggle into which we might be drawn'.

The Chancellor 'submitted to' the Prime Minister 'Mr Asquith a memorandum urging that a truce should be declared between the Parties for the purpose of securing the cooperation of our leading party statesmen in a settlement of our national problems'. These included 'the development of our agricultural resources, National Training for Defence, the remedying of social evils' and a re-haul of public expenditure. The plan was supported by the Liberal Party Ministers Lord Crewe, Sir Edward Grey, Lord Haldane and Winston Churchill; and also by the Tories Lord Lansdowne, Lord Cawdor, Lord Curzon, Walter Long and Austen Chamberlain – but it foundered on opposition from the backbenchers in both parties.[8]

The case of Ireland

Ireland became a part of the United Kingdom in 1801 – though both the Scots Presbyterian settlers in the north east and the Catholics were without any vote at that time, and the country was run by an Anglo-Irish elite, while much of its land was owned by Lords who lived in England. Rents raised by absentee landlords rose from £732,200 in 1779 to between six and seven million in 1845.[9] By 1870 four fifths of profitable land was owned by less than 4,000 people, and one tenth owned by just 20 families. The Irish tenants raised little rent for their landlords, who forced them off, until famine killed 985,366 people; 84,123 families were evicted during the famine itself.[10] Judged surplus to requirements 1.5 million of Ireland's people emigrated in the aftermath of the famine – helots in England's burgeoning industrial cities; 40,000 were transported to Australia as convicts, or they went to the United States, almost five million between 1830 and 1914, until by 1890 two of every five Irish-born people were living abroad. The population fell from 8.2 million in 1841 to 6.5 million in 1851.

In July 1920, Sir Warren Fisher, the Permanent Secretary to the Treasury, explained to Bonar Law that 'for centuries we exploited the country, and when we didn't do that we prevented her development lest it should damage our own undertakings'.[11]

Union did not favour Ireland's indigenous industries in the south where wool and cotton weaving were wiped out by competition from England; but it did boost the north east, where linen and later shipbuilding and some engineering prospered on access to British markets. In the first place the northern Protestant settlers had the advantage of secure tenure that was denied to Catholics in the south, and encouraged the cottage industry of linen weaving. In 1910 there were more linen spindles in use in Belfast alone than in any country in the world, and Belfast's York Street Flax Spinning Mill was the largest linen mill in the world. Engineering grew up to serve the linen mills with firms like James Mackie's.[12] British investors promoted a shift to heavy industry. In 1911 there were 350,000 living in Belfast, and 300,000 in the capital, Dublin, which was largely an administrative and commercial city. In 1907 industries in the Belfast region made up £19.1 million of the £20.9 million manufactured goods (excluding food and drink) exported from the whole of Ireland.

The social question in Ireland was greatly shaped by the relation to Britain, which overall stunted industrial development, apart from in Ulster, principally in Belfast and Lisburn. In 1911 the census recorded a population of 4.3 million, of whom just over 3 million lived in the countryside. In 1870 Karl Marx would write that 'in Ireland the land question has been up to now the exclusive form of the social question because it is a question of existence, of life and death, for the immense majority of the Irish people', adding that 'it is at the same time inseparable from the national question'. A worldwide fall in the prices of farm goods hurt Irish tenant farmers in 1879 and many were unable to pay their rents and were evicted. Michael Davitt's Land League was founded to fight for tenants' rights, and supported by the Irish MP Charles Stewart Parnell. It took up tactics like the isolation of Captain Boycott, and its supporters assassinated the Earl of Antrim in 1878 and Viceroy Lord Frederick Cavendish and Under Secretary Burke in 1882. Land Leaguers including Davitt were imprisoned, but Gladstone also brought in measures to protect tenants and even to help them buy the farms they worked.

Over time the lot of the Irish farmer improved. As in England, the aristocracy sold off its land to meet its debts, and small and middle-sized farmers set up in business. These farmers were Ireland's business class, later joined by the Dublin-based commercial companies.

Throughout the 19th century the United Kingdom struggled with the question of democracy, very gradually enlarging the male franchise, in painfully slow steps: the Reform Acts of 1832 (which gave the vote to the propertied urban middle classes), 1867 (which gave the vote to working-class heads of households in towns), and 1884 (which extended the 1867 act to the countryside). Women had to wait for the vote until well into the 20th century, in two reforms of 1918 and 1928. These historical dates and parliamentary acts cover a great social struggle through which the sphere of civil society was gradually enlarged to encompass more groups of people, as they proved their rights through protest on the one hand, and responsible moderation on the other. Alongside the right to vote the civil liberties of people were slowly enlarged, with freedom from arrest, freedom of conscience, the right to organise, and a free press. All these freedoms meant that more people were incorporated into civil society, through that negotiating process of *reform*, and so trusted with greater freedoms.

Though Ireland was a part of the United Kingdom from 1801, and in principle the same laws applied, the different social conditions meant that the laws on both political rights and civil rights worked differently – like a white linen tablecloth set down, not on a smooth Chippendale table top, but a rough-hewn wooden board. Westminster's successive rules of who was in and who was out were drawn from English conditions and suppositions about what property qualification would work in favour of which constituency. These were the negotiations that were had out in the debates over reform. Applied to Ireland they often worked differently, because they did not arise out of social conditions in Ireland.

The main difference was that a large, rural population had its own church, ideas about schooling and marriage and language in some places; while another congregational group in the north east were mostly Presbyterian Protestants, more urbanised, and closer in culture to Britain, the more stridently they set themselves apart from the Irish Catholics. When the First Reform Act of 1832 was enacted, it tended only to enshrine the rights of the existing Anglo-Irish elite, and a smaller group of Catholics and Non-Conformists who had the means (Feargus O'Connor was elected to represent County Cork in 1835, but disqualified for not meeting the property qualification). The Act of 1867, applying first to urban areas, had some impact. But the most dramatic changes came about with the Act of 1884, extending to rural districts, which managed to greatly enlarge both the number of Catholic voters in the south, and the Presbyterian voters in the north. These changes, though, were not debated and managed according to Irish conditions, and did not reflect the same consensus.

One clear mark of the difference was that Parliament made special laws just for Ireland. There were a whole set of laws, nicely called the Coercion Acts, passed between 1832 and 1881, that gave the authorities powers over a community whose loyalty could not be counted upon. These were laws passed to put down rural social movements that attacked landlords and other not-quite-legal and somewhat secretive groups, like Daniel O'Connell's Land League, the Whiteboys and Ribbonmen before them, and after the Fenians and the Irish Republican Brotherhood. Thousands were penalised under these laws – not different in kind from the laws that were set down to fight

Luddites and other rebels in England, but directed at local problems, and lasting rather longer into the 19th and even 20th century.

As there were different sticks to beat the disloyal population, there were different carrots to win them over, too. The British elite was well-accomplished in ruling through intermediaries that it recruited from its challengers. Catholic Emancipation in 1828 and 1829 was passed to lift the ban that kept Daniel O'Connell from taking the County Clare seat he won in the election. Since 1795 the British government had paid a small amount towards the costs of a Catholic Seminary, St Patrick's at Maynooth, but Robert Peel chose to face down opposition in 1845 to increase the sum to a more realistic £26,000. In 1871 William Ewart Gladstone went further disestablishing the Church of Ireland, and making a grant of £1,000,000 to the College at Maynooth. Then, in the 1880s, as we have seen, the British government brought in land reform that let Irish farmers buy the land they worked.

Britain related differently to the Protestant Settlers in the north east. Written into the Act of Union was an ideal of a Protestant Ascendancy, the establishment of the Church of Ireland, and the preferential treatment of its Anglo-Irish adherents. By analogy, those rights were mirrored in the relation between the elite and the Protestant Scots-Irish settlers of Ulster. The 'Ulster Custom' was that the protestant farmers of Ulster would have security of tenure, and even the right to sell their right to tenure. Long-established it was given the force of law in 1870. Carried over into the new industrial order in Belfast the Ulster Custom translated into a promise of Protestant Jobs in a Protestant State.

It is worth making the comparison with Scotland to ask why Union was a relative success there, but sharply contested in Ireland. In both states the Anglican elite in Westminster cooperated with a Presbyterian, mostly lower-middle class community of farmers and craftsmen. In both cases the tie that bound them was a struggle against a third party. The lowland Scots fought a long conflict against a Highland Gaelic society and culture alongside the British; the Ulster Protestants fought for and defended the interests of the Crown against Catholic Ireland. The major difference is that the Scottish highlanders were effectively defeated and dispersed as a culture, abandoning their Catholic faith, dispossessed from the land, and often dragooned into the army to fight in England's wars against America; as valiantly as the Scots settlers fought for King William at the Boyne, their victory over the Celtic countryside was never as definitive. Highland culture was defanged, and once made harmless it was re-incorporated into the national identity as a motif of Scottishness, while the highlanders themselves were removed and made a proletariat in the new towns. Scots shared in Britain's successes, and played a key role in the British Empire, not least in settling Ulster, but also in Imperial Companies like William Mackinnon's British East Africa Company, and in the British Army, which boasted many proud Scots Regiments. Ulster's Protestants also shared in Britain's successes, fighting in Britain's wars, and trading in the Empire, as William and Alexander MacArthur did. But Ireland's Catholic population did not enjoy those same privileges. Catholics did serve in the British Army, though more often as ordinary troops than as officers.

The British elite established different relations between the largely rural and southern Catholic population, and the increasingly urban and Protestant people in the north east. These different stances collided with the democratisation of the British state, as the enlarged vote heightened the contest for popular support in Ireland.

Charles Stewart Parnell, himself a landlord and a Protestant, had joined agitation over a new Irish Land League in the late 1870s. Joined in Parliament by Catholic Irishmen elected under the 1884 franchise, Parnell was wooed by William Ewart Gladstone's offer of Home Rule for Ireland, and he organised his peers as the Home Rule Party. Conservative Party leader Sir Randolph Churchill wrote that he 'had decided some time ago that if the Grand Old Man', i.e. Gladstone, 'went for Home Rule, the Orange card would be the one to play', to get the support of the northern Protestants. Churchill's plan even succeeded in splitting the Liberal Party, as many Liberals became 'Liberal Unionists'. Britain's Liberal and Conservative parties were having their differences out in Ireland, greatly dramatising and accentuating the contest between the faith groups, now reconstituted as Home Rulers and Unionists. It was a dynamic that further entrenched hostilities, cementing the Protestant reaction.

Home Rule provoked a near-hysterical reaction from Tories and from the Orange Order in Ulster. To them 'Home Rule' was 'Rome Rule'. But it was really quite a modest reform. What the Irish Party leaders Parnell, and then later Redmond, were being offered was only a measure of devolution that fell short even of the Responsible Self-Government under the Crown enjoyed by the Dominions like New Zealand, Australia and Canada. They were only being offered a degree of self-government within the United Kingdom. The measure was meant to contain the pressure for separation. It was comparable to the native administration that the Empire offered to African peoples under the 'Dual Mandate'. Without the military mobilisation of Ulster against Home Rule, it is unlikely that there would have been Irish Volunteers, or a rising in Dublin in 1916.

Jim Larkin and the Dublin lockout

The great conflict in Ireland before the war was not over sovereignty but the rights of workers. Liverpool Irish labour organiser Jim Larkin founded the Irish Transport and General Workers Union, which was pitched into a militant struggle with the Dublin employers in 1913.

All across the United Kingdom in the 1870s there had been a revival in trade unionism, with the emergence of 'New Model Unions' of the semi- and un-skilled challenging the 'Old Gang' of craft unions who controlled the Trade Union Congress. The strike of the match girls at the Bryant and May factory, and the founding of the Boilermakers' and Gas-workers' Unions. The older craft unions worked mostly as friendly societies, paying out benefits to members in hardship, while the newer unions fought not just for better wages, but also for an eight-hour day – an issue that divided the new unions and the Old Gang at the Trades Union Congress in 1890. In Britain the tensions between the 'Old Gang' of craft union leaders and the New Unionism was contained, and the mood of insurrection that the newer activist brought was moderated. Later, many of the full-time officials who were taken on by the new unions were themselves veterans of the older craft tradition, making a moderate trade union bureaucracy.

In Ireland the clash between craft unions and new model unions was much harsher. The artisan guilds in the 18th century had been monopolised by Protestant Irishmen to the exclusion of their Catholic countrymen. These craft restrictions were carried over into the organisation of craft unions in the Linen, engineering and ship-building industries in the north east. 'There was nothing unusual, anywhere, in a skilled craftsman's securing the entry of his son to the trade', writes Austen Morgan, 'but it was only in Ulster, with its sectarian political culture, that it became a grievance related to the national question'.[13] Linen workers struck in 1893 asking not to work alongside a Catholic. In Harland and Wolff's shipyards workers struck against their Catholic fellows in 1864. Many trades were associated with lodges of the Orange Order, a society dedicated to protecting Protestant interests in Ulster.

Because of the way that men of the Protestant faith predominated in skilled trades and their unions, Catholic wage labourers tended to get less skilled work, as labourers, porters, in transport, on farms and dairies. Before 1900 they were markedly unorganised. But in 1908 James Larkin founded the Irish Transport and General Workers Union. Pointedly, the ITGWU was set up as a breakaway from the Liverpool-based National Union of Dock Labourers, which had united Catholic and Protestant workers in a strike centred on Belfast under Larkin's leadership the previous year. But the other NUDL leaders resisted Larkin's pitch to recruit Irish workers, expelled him, and even had him prosecuted for misdirecting NUDL funds to strikers who had left to join the ITGWU.

Jim Larkin in the 1913 Dublin lock-out

Larkin's new model union had some good wins for the carters and railwaymen in 1910, and it grew quickly recruiting 10,000. A resolute attack on Larkin and the ITGWU was organised by William O'Brien, who persuaded other employers to join him in a 'lock out' of those workplaces that were unionised. The struggle was vast and bitter, lasting thirteen weeks, with violent clashes.

On Bloody Friday hundreds of police attacked a strikers' rally, chasing people down Princes Street, and even into their homes. The strike was notable for the setting up, by Captain Jack White, of the Irish Citizens Army to defend the strikers against attacks, Europe's first workers' militia. 'Hitherto the workers of Ireland have fought as parts of the armies led by their masters', wrote the socialist James Connolly, 'never as a member of any army officered, trained and inspired by men of their own class'. Solidarity from the grassroots of the British labour movement raised £100,000. When railwaymen in Britain blacked goods from Ireland, 2000 of them were in dispute with the employers. The full-time officials of the British labour movement, though, were scared by the rank and file action. National Union of Railwaymen leader Jimmy Thomas stamped down on the unofficial action, and at a special meeting of TUC officials on 9 December 1913 Larkin was refused support, and told instead to let the parliamentary representatives mediate a settlement. The strikers went back defeated.

Putting the gun into Irish politics

'Landlordism in Ireland is maintained solely by the English Army', Marx wrote. Joseph Chamberlain thought that the British system in Ireland was 'founded on the bayonets of 30,000 soldiers encamped permanently in a hostile country'.

A military camp in the Curragh, County Kildare was in 1893 manned by the 1st Battalion Royal Irish Regiment, the 1st Battalion Lancashire Fusiliers, and the 2nd Battalion Worcestershire Regiment. Between 1901 and 1902 nine counties and two cities were put under emergency rule and thirteen MPs sent to jail for agitating over land.

By 1904 over 34,000 troops were garrisoned in the country, more than 25,000 of them in the south. They were mostly British troops, and to stop them making friends in Ireland, they were regularly rotated.[14]

As Britain's industrial towns recruited surplus Irishmen, so did the British Army. The Royal Irish Regiment with its headquarters in Dublin sent regiments to fight the Maori in 1863 and the Boers in 1899, and to help rule over India and Egypt. Military service in the British Army was an escape from rural poverty for many. But the militarisation of Unionism was a terrible threat to the people.

Over and above the official military forces, Ulster's Protestant settlers were united in an Orange Order that used force against the rebellious Irish. When the Liberal Prime Minister Gladstone made a tentative offer of Home Rule, English Tories united with the Orangemen to fight it.

Home Rule was again raised by Irish MPs in Westminster, but while their leader John Redmond debated with liberal leader Herbert Asquith Britain's imperialists made common cause with the Ulster Protestants to fight it.

On 23 September 1911, Sir Edward Carson, a judge and an Attorney General from Dublin, told the gathered Orangemen at Captain Craig's estate Craigavon that 'we will yet defeat the most nefarious conspiracy that has ever been hatched against a free people'. Carson was backed by Lord Alfred Milner, architect of Britain's imperial policy, Major General Henry Wilson, Director of Military Operations at the War Office and Tory leader Andrew Bonar Law. On 9 April 1912, 100,000 Ulster Volunteers were drilled before Carson and Bonar Law.

In March of 1914, asked to prepare for the possibility of taking action against the Ulster Volunteer Force, the British garrison in the Curragh threatened mutiny, led by Brigadier-General Sir Hubert Gough, his three Colonels and 55 of his officers in the Third Cavalry Brigade. General Henry Wilson called on Bonar Law demanding he 'back Gough'. On 23 March Gough and his officers went to London where they were promised by Sir John French and Secretary of State for War Sir John Seely that 'the troops under our command will not be called upon to enforce the present Home Rule Bill in Ulster'.[15]

On 25 April 1914 Carson got a telegram carrying one word: 'Lion'. It was the signal that 10,000 new Mannlicher rifles, 9,100 Mauser rifles, and two million rounds of ammunition for the Ulster Volunteers had been landed at Larne. They were bought at Hamburg with £45,640 raised by Carson and Milner.

In response to Carson's Ulster Volunteer Force, the Irish Nationalist Party leader John Redmond sanctioned the mobilisation of an Irish National Volunteer Force – that numbered 168,000 at its height. The point of the National Volunteers was in the first instance as a counterweight to the UVF and to protect Home Rule. While the parading of the Ulster Volunteers was sanctioned, the National Volunteers were closely watched by the police.

Though it has its own details and drives, the militarisation of Ireland was not at all unique. The whole of Europe and all her colonies were being dragooned up and down, sabres rattled and revolts threatened.

Kitchener's Orange army

In building his army to fight the Great War, Lord Kitchener drew on the traditions of the British Army, and those were above all Royalist, Tory and Orange. In their backgrounds the senior officers were often either brought up or trained in Ireland.

Secretary of State for War Lord Kitchener was born in Ireland in 1850, son of an English officer from East Anglia 'who had been brought up to regard himself as the member of a Protestant master race in an alien, hostile and superstitious land'.[16]

The first Commander-in-Chief of the British Expeditionary Force Sir John French was of the DeFreyne family that had owned estates in Roscommon since the 14th century. In 1918 he was made Lord Lieutenant of Ireland, or military dictator.

Chief of the Imperial General Staff Sir Henry Hughes Wilson was born in County Longford, to a land-owning family that traced its residence back to 1690. Wilson was a supporter of the Orange Order and the organiser of the Curragh Mutiny.

Field Marshal Lord Roberts was a committed Unionist and also a supporter of the mutiny.

Commander of the Fifth Army, Sir Hubert de la Poer Gough, though born in London was from an Anglo-Irish family that settled in 1600 and became landowners in Gurteen, County Wexford. He played a leading role in the Curragh Mutiny.

The Home Rule crisis as a cause of war

As we have seen, Lloyd George outlined a severe challenge to Westminster Government in 1910, but we left one challenge off the list – arguably the most important: Ireland. Today's historians tell the story of the Great War as being triggered by obscure events in far-off Sarajevo, or perhaps as a consequence of militarism (usually meaning only German militarism). But Lloyd George includes a cause that historians like Max Hastings and Hew Strachan make little play of.

'The long-drawn out and wearisome tragedy of the relations between Great Britain and Ireland played an important part in the World War', wrote the wartime Chancellor and Prime Minister. What he means is that being tied up in Ireland, Britain was at the mercy of her allies.

There can be no doubt that the expectation on the continent that Britain had for the moment sunk so deep into the quagmires of the Irish bog as to be unable to extract her feet in time to march eastward was one of the considerations that encouraged Germany to guarantee Austria unconditional support in her Serbian adventure.

Shifting the blame onto Austria and her 'Serbian adventure' Lloyd George does not quite see that Ireland was to Britain what Serbia was to Austria and Germany. Like Serbia, Ireland was a small nation clamouring for her freedom; and like Serbia, Ireland was a field on which the militarists of the greater power worked out their anger. Like Serbia's claims for independence, Ireland's were made into the excuse for a pointless act of sabre-rattling by the reactionary tendency in the Metropolitan nation.

The politicisation of the Irish Question by the Liberal and Tory parties found them championing the rival factions of Home Rulers and Ulster Unionists. As the two rival forces, the Ulster Volunteer Force and the Irish Volunteers, the struggle of Tory and Liberal were being played out in Ireland as a military contest. The Tories and their Generals saw Ireland and the place where British Patriotism would be proved higher than mere parliamentary majorities. As Lloyd George explains 'the last days of July 1914 found the traditional British parties confronting each other in the fiercest political conflict waged since the suppression of the last Jacobite uprising'.

Piling on the parallels, Lloyd George said that 'we were faced with the prospect of an internecine struggle which would have rent the nation into warring factions such as these islands had not witnessed since the great Civil Wars'. Even more alarming was that 'there was no surety that if bloodshed ensued its flow could have been confined to Ireland'. To Lloyd George it seemed that the Irish conflict would trigger a social conflagration on the British mainland: 'there are towns on this side of the Channel where it would have been difficult to keep the peace among the votaries of warring creeds if their fellow religionists in Ireland on either side were slain'. Whether urban Britain would truly have lurched into rebellion over Ireland, the Chancellor's fears of disorder in Britain had a real basis, as the social turmoil of 1910–11 showed.

Just as the Curragh Mutiny and the Redmondite parading were approaching a climax in the summer of 1914, they were suddenly deflated by the war.

Meanwhile in Sarajevo

As Ireland's troubles were amplified in the British Parliament, so too were the Balkan wars resonating in Vienna and Berlin. Serbia's leaders had leveraged the modest self-government they enjoyed under Turkish rule into full-blown independence by turning on their Ottoman rulers in 1873 – only to be denied the incorporation of Bosnia into Serbia by Austria's land grab. Sir Lewis Namier explained the importance of small nations in inter-imperialist rivalries by analogy to Britain's difficulties in Ireland: 'Consider the amount of disturbance which during the nineteenth century was caused in the political life of this country by Ireland', he wrote, 'and you can gauge the effect which two dozen Irelands were bound to have on the life of nineteenth-century Europe as borderlands between contending nations'.[17]

The Balkan Wars of 1911 and 1912 saw Serbia, with Russian support, shore up its position. To Kaiser Wilhelm the challenge of 'Slavdom' was a threat to 'Germandom'. 'We will not leave Austria in the lurch', he told the Swiss Ambassador in December 1912: 'if diplomacy fails we shall have to fight this racial war'.[18]

On 28 June 1914, Gavrilo Princip, Muhamed Mehmedbašić and Nedeljko Čabrinović of the Young Bosnia group attacked and killed the Archduke Ferdinand, along with his wife and driver. The audacious assassination provoked fury in Vienna at Serbia's agitation against Austria. A demand that Serbia put its police and government under Austrian direction in the suppression of nationalist sentiment – the July Ultimatum – was too humiliating for the Serbs to accept. Germany's ambition for a forward policy in the Balkans found them goading Vienna on to humiliate the Serbs. Russia, anticipating an attack on Serbia, mobilised its troops to the German borders in the East. Meanwhile, France, fearing Germany's militancy, and committed to supporting Russia, mobilised its troops to the border on Germany's south.

Like its allies, France and Russia, Britain had long been hostile to Germany's expanding influence in the Balkans. The German

Ambassador in London asked Sir Edward Grey whether Britain would act if Germany attacked France, but he did not say so. As Bertrand Russell pointed out at the time, Grey hid the truth that Britain was secretly committed to supporting France, leading Germany to think that they could act against France without a British response. So it was that Germany, overconfident, sent its army through Belgium to attack France.

Seventy-five years later, US Ambassador April Glaspie, when asked if Iraq had the 'green light' to invade Kuwait, would assure Saddam Hussein's Foreign Minister that America had 'no opinion on these Arab-Arab conflicts' – though in fact they had already drawn up detailed plans for a war against Iraq. Saddam walked right into the trap. Glaspie was just following Sir Edward Grey's playbook.

In 1914 the British Government revealed their plan to use the invasion of Belgium as a reason for starting war against Germany. According to Russell, 'the neutrality of Belgium, the integrity of France and her colonies, and the naval defence of the northern and western costs of France were mere pretexts'. Writing in *Justice*, Glasgow socialist John Maclean agreed: 'Sir Edward Grey only had to wait until Belgium's neutrality had been broken to seize the "moral" excuse for Britain taking up arms'.[19]

Just as the national chauvinism of the German people was excited by the government's jingoism, the years imbuing the British people with hatred of Germany manifested themselves in a great upsurge of popular demand for war:

during the first four days of August 1914 I shall never forget the warlike crowds that thronged Whitehall and poured in to Downing Street, whilst the Cabinet was deliberating on the alternative of peace or war … multitudes of young people concentrated in Westminster demonstrating for war against Germany.

The London demonstrations had their counterparts in St Petersburg, Berlin, Vienna, and Paris.[20]

Europe was a powder keg, and the July Ultimatum was the spark that lit it.

The Great War as a magical, but temporary, resolution to social conflict

In the summer of 1914, recall that British politics was deadlocked, and the whole nation rocked by a violent stand-off in Ireland. What was the effect of the war? Here is Lloyd George again:

> Then there came a real war, like a mighty rushing wind, the struggle not of sects and factions, but nations and continents, and the incipient fires of civil war were swept into the great conflagration.

The Chancellor remembered that just before the outbreak of war, the then-Prime Minister Asquith 'had been howled down by Unionist members'. But with the declaration of war against Germany 'the same members were cheering to the rafters': 'In the course of a single day angry political passions were silenced and followed by the just wrath' of patriotism. And, as he had hoped back in 1910, with the memorandum proposing government by Statesmen, with the declaration of war, 'party politics and party bitterness disappeared'.

On 30 July 1914, Asquith said 'in the interests of the whole world that this country should present a united front … I speak and act with the authority of an undivided nation'. Then on 31 August Asquith's 'undivided nation' hardened up into a demand for obedience:

> Here we are, all sections of us, happily united, as the people of these islands have never been before, in the common determi-

nation each to play his own part and all to play the part of the whole, and that at such a moment we should be indulging in acrimonious discussions on a matter of domestic politics, however important, is, I think, of the worst possible omen.

Dissent was to be outlawed. Lord Lansdowne moved 'a Bill to suspend proceedings upon certain controversial legislation during the continuance of war' – here was Lloyd George's fantasy of the suspension of political contestation, now proposed in law.

The determination that there should be no dissent was not just aimed at Ireland but at all of the country. The idea was that all social conflict should be set aside for the greater good. Given the social tensions in Britain – and indeed the tensions in all the European powers – the exigency of war it was hoped would silence all challenges to the authority of the elite.

Where the establishment had been rocked by a Great Unrest in the years 1910 to 1913, peace broke out on the domestic front, just as war broke out in between nations. Rebellious labour was quieted. Arthur Henderson took over the leadership of the Labour Party and brokered a Treasury Agreement with the Trades Unions that promised flexibility and an end to 'restrictive practices' and strikes – for which he was rewarded with a seat in the Cabinet. The Treasury Agreement was set down in law as the Munitions of War Act, under which a munitions worker could not leave his job without a certificate from his employer (to build trust with the union officials the government also created Munitions Tribunals to moderate any complaints).

An 'Appeal to Free Men' published by the Trade Union Congress Parliamentary Committee on 7 October 1915 hoped that the war would 'secure such a victory as will free the world from the fear of that military tyranny which Germany would impose upon it'. 'From the beginning of the War until the end', wrote Sidney Webb, 'the Labour Party stuck at nothing in its determination to help the Government win the war'.

Christabel Pankhurst made her peace with the government, too. The Women's Social and Political Union suspended their campaign for the duration, and put their efforts instead into a 'white feather' campaign of shaming those who refused to fight. The Suffragette was renamed The Britannia.

In 1917 Lionel Curtis, an influential government official and historian of Empire, looked back on what had happened, judging that the country

> was four years ago on the brink of civil war. And if the Germans had not saved us the struggle would have raged not only between Catholic and Protestant Ireland but throughout Great Britain between class and class.[21]

The moderating impact of war upon social conflict was felt across Europe. Asquith's French counterpart Poincaré declared a *union sacrée*, and 'all divisions in the nation disappeared'.[22] In Germany the many Social Democrat deputies voted the funds to fight the war. All through the 20th century the Socialist International had committed itself to opposing the war, and made plans to organise a great general strike to paralyse the war when it came. But in that autumn of 1914 they learned that the warmongers had, for the moment, won over the peoples of Europe to fight. As Ruth Dudley Edwards explains, among the socialist parties, 'only Lenin's Bolsheviks, the Serbs and the Irish remained true to the resolutions' of the Socialist International. 'That the Irish did so owed much to the intransigent stance of Larkin and Connolly':

> "Stop at home", said Larkin. "Arm for Ireland. Fight for Ireland and no other land."[23]

Those socialists who did not rally to the cause of war, Lenin and Trotsky in Russia, Karl Liebknecht and Rosa Luxemburg in

Germany, John MacLean in Scotland and James Connolly in Dublin, were isolated. Some, like Liebknecht and Luxemburg, would be thrown in prison to silence them. French socialist Jean Jaures, who had done most to prepare against the war, was shot on its eve. But the European socialist leaders, their loyalty to the state having been built up through gas-and-water socialist reforms, preferred to wrap themselves in their respective national flags.

Social conformity was assured in Britain through two measures. First, was the Defence of the Realm Act, under which 'No person shall by word of mouth or in writing spread reports likely to cause disaffection or alarm among any of His Majesty's forces or among the civilian population'. John Maclean was the first person arrested under DORA, and later William Gallacher and Bertrand Russell would be imprisoned along with many others. The second measure, brought in for the first time in January 1916, was conscription, agreed in a secret session of Parliament, forcing men to sign up for the army, unless they were infirm or in vital occupations.

Social peace meant the suspension of the Home Rule conflict, too. The legislation was all suspended. The promise that Home Rule would be brought in after the war quieted the Nationalists, while Unionists were promised that Ulster would be left out – and the argument over those terms was stopped by the 'greater cause'.

Nowhere was the stifling of dissent under the common good clearer than over Ireland. 'Armed Nationalist Catholics in the South will be only too glad to join arms with the armed Protestant Ulstermen in the North', said the Irish Nationalist Leader John Redmond. 'Is it too much to hope that out of this situation there may spring a result which will be good not merely for the Empire but good for the future welfare and integrity of the Irish Nation?' he asked.

Redmond's position was to earn for Ireland the respect of

having fought for Britain. He said:

> no people can be said to have rightly proved their nationhood and their power to maintain it until they have demonstrated their military prowess; and though Irish blood has reddened the earth of every continent, never until now have we as a people set a national army in the field.

This was in a propaganda pamphlet, *The Irish at the Front*, published in 1916 and circulated by the Department of Recruiting in Ireland, which sent copies out to every household in Waterford.

Redmond's hope that Irishmen would earn respect from the British Government and people by their sacrifice was not so strange. 100,000 Jews joined the German armed forces after an appeal by a Berlin Synagogue; 370,000 black Americans were inducted into the American army after more than one million responded to calls to join up. Military service and civil rights were connected. Redmond's hopes for the recognition of the Irish people, though, would founder on the British establishment's belief that they could not govern the Empire if they gave up Ireland.

Irishmen in the British Army

Thousands upon thousands of Irish men have served in the British Army over the centuries. On the rough calculation that one quarter of them were Catholic, mostly Irish, the British Expeditionary Force in 1914 had twelve Catholic chaplains; by 1915 the Church of England share rose sharply and the Catholic fell.[24]

There were three Divisions raised in Ireland in the Great War, the 36th (Ulster) Division, the 10th (Irish) Division and the 16th (Irish) Division. Up to 15 December 1915, 85,068 men were enlisted in Ireland, of whom 45,123 were Catholics and 39,502 were Protestants. The Ulster Volunteers sent 24,638. John Redmond's Irish National Volunteers recruited 18,613.[25]

All told 206,000 Irishmen fought in the Great War – and 49,500 men of the Irish Regiments in the British Army were killed – around ten times as many as were killed in Ireland from the Rising in 1916 to the end of the Civil War in 1923. The men that John Redmond marshalled, the National Volunteers, and those he recruited afterwards mostly went to the 16th and 10th Divisions. Carson's Ulster Volunteer Force made up the 36th. The Irish Catholic recruits were mostly unskilled labourers, and, against common belief, mostly from urban areas, like Dublin and Waterford.

The point is often made today, looking back at the Easter Rising, that more Irish men served in the British Army than came out in 1916. That is true. How were they treated? John Redmond, who did so much to raise the 16th Division, was sorry that it was under the command of Sir Lawrence Worthington Parsons, whose family were the landowners of Birr, in County Offaly, when it was called Parsonstown. Parsons, who came out of retirement to put the stamp of Unionism on the 16th Division, praised its Catholic troops:

> the devotions of those rough Irishmen to myself and their commanding officers, all of us Unionists and Protestants, shows what can be done with the Irish peasantry if properly handled with firmness and sympathy.[26]

John Hamilton Maxwell Staniforth was an Oxford graduate and officer to the 6th Connaught Rangers. He saw his men more frankly as

> about a dozen seedy, ragged, lousy, unshaven tramps who lurched in and lay on their cots smoking, spitting, quarrelling, making water all over the room ... hiccupping and vomiting.

It was after three before the last of them settled into a repulsive lousy slumber.[27]

Prime Minister Lloyd George despaired at Lord Kitchener's contempt for his Irish recruits. 'With extraordinary tactlessness, old officers were let loose on Munster, Connaught and Leinster to lure men to the colours to the strains of "God Save the King"'. Kitchener 'approved the embroidery of the Red Hand of Ulster on the banner of the Northern Division, but banned the Irish Harp on the Southern'.[28] John Redmond pleaded for a divisional badge for the Irish volunteers, but Sir Lawrence demurred, appealing to the traditions of the regiments from before the raising of the Irish Volunteers. He explained that when he lectured the men 'the origins and history of the regiment is explained to them, why they have a sphinx on their badge, a tiger, or an elephant etc.' 'This instils *esprit de corps*', he said.[29]

Redmond tried to fast-track some southern Catholic officers into post, and in the Ninth Munsters the figure even reached one third. English officers like Staniforth complained that 'there's altogether too much politics in this Irish Brigade business'. Irish Protestants and British Officers were drafted in to command the Irishmen, a 'horde of English cockneys who never understood Irishmen, or how to treat them decently', thought Captain Daniel Sheehan; they were 'blatantly antagonistic' to the Irish cause.

'It is these soldiers of ours', Redmond said in the pamphlet *The Irish at the Front*, 'carrying with them their green flags and their Irish war pipes', who were 'offering up the supreme sacrifice of life with a smile on their lips because it was given for Ireland'. The truth was harsher. The 10th Division had real successes at the battle for Wytschaete, celebrated in a propaganda film as 'North and South Irishmen fighting side by side'. They had fought well at the Battle of Loos in 1915, though total British losses were 22,504 killed and 35,641 wounded. Already some in Ireland were asking why their losses were not featuring in the war reports.

Worse was to come with the struggle to take the Gallipoli Peninsula from the Turks, beginning in April 1915. On 25 April the First Munsters were in the 29th Division which landed on the beach in the River Clyde, a transport ship. The men were disembarked in range of the defenders guns at great loss of life, and a retreat. An officer in the Royal Munster Fusiliers recalled that the men 'were just mown down in scores into a bleeding silence as they showed themselves at the Clyde's open hatches'. It was, he said, 'pure butchery'. On 6 August the 29th Brigade of the 10th (Irish) Division were sent with Australian and New Zealand Units landing at an Anzac Cove into fierce fighting. The Division's remaining Brigades were landed at Suvla Bay that day and the next. Redmond said 'already we have seen in the casualty list the toll which has been paid by these gallant brothers of ours from the Curragh and from Dublin'. Criticism of the Gallipoli campaign only got harsher as more news came out; it was widely seen as a disaster, and Australians and Irishmen were sickened by the sacrifice.

John Redmond's Irish Parliamentary Party lost Tyrone MP Thomas Kettle who had enrolled as a Lieutenant in the Dublin Fusiliers at the front in 1916; and then in June 1917 Major Willie Redmond, younger brother of John, MP for East Clare, was killed on the front line.

As impressive as Redmond's early recruiting efforts had been, the numbers signing up were dwindling by 1916. In Parliament Colonel Craig rebutted the Redmondite claims that the Irish had shouldered more than their share:

If you take what has been done in England and strike an average of what Ireland has done you will find that the response that has been made to the recruiting agents in Ireland has been a disgrace to a large portion of that part of the country.

Craig pointed out that 'the old historical Irish regiments were being depleted and being filled up by Englishmen and Scotsmen' (House of Commons, 3 May 1916). It was a bitter truth. The 10th and 16th Divisions would have to be amalgamated, as the sacrifice of Irish lives grew, while the eagerness of the recruiting dwindled.

The Ulster Volunteers suffered terribly, too. The Ulster Division was sent to France in October 1915, and came to a bloody end in a most gallant attack at Thiepval in July 1916. Jim Maultsaid wrote in his diary about the Inniskillings: 'some of the Skins wore Orange sashes, rushing at the Germans shouting "No surrender!"'[30] At the end of the day on 1 July, in the Battle of the Somme, the 36th (Ulster) Division had suffered over 4,900 casualties: 86 officers and 1,983 other ranks killed or missing; 102 officers and 2,626 other ranks wounded. In letters, men described the horror. One wrote:

A 9th Inniskilling is lying at the top of the trench and he has a bullet through his steel hat. He rolls over into the trenches at my feet. He is an awful sight. His brain is oozing out of the side of his head and he is calling his pal with an occasional cry of "Billy Grey, will you not come to me?"[31]

According to Jim Maultsaid 'the list grows as everyone still remembers that terrible journey through the human debris of the battlefield, the dressing stations, base hospital and finally – Old Blighty!'[32]

The impact of the Ulster Volunteers' casualties, though, was different from that of the national volunteers. Where the loyalty of Ulster was affirmed by the sacrifice of their volunteers, the suffering of the Irishmen only seemed to underscore the futility of fighting for the British Empire, and their second-class status under it.

For all the men who were killed or wounded, brutalised and

abused, in whichever division, the war was a pointless slaughter. The real heroes of the Great War were not the recruiting sergeants John Redmond and Edward Carson, but those who fought against the war.

The horror of war

The suffering of the Irish Divisions in Belgium and the Dardanelles was sadly not unique. The Great War was for its time an unprecedented slaughter. 'It is our strength, our hope, which is being mowed down in swathes like grass', wrote Rosa Luxemburg.[33]

From the Allied Headquarters Major Charteris wrote in the winter of 1914 that

General Rice our senior sapper has made the most original forecast of all! He predicts that neither we nor the Germans will be able to break through a strongly defended and entrenched line, and that gradually the line will extend from the sea to Switzerland, and the war will end in stalemate.

So it did. For all the attempts to break through, the armies, once they formed up, barely moved, pounding each other from their respective positions, digging in.

'It was impossible to dig deeper than eighteen inches without finding water, and along whole stretches of the line garrisons had to do their stint waist high', according to Alan Clark. Worse: 'the wounded who collapsed into the slime would often drown, unnoticed in the heat of some local engagement, and lie concealed for days until their bodies, porous from decomposition, would rise once again to the surface'. Harold Eagles was buried in a pit of mud and the bodies of his own comrades, and would never talk about it afterwards. Nurse Mairi Chisholm wrote in her diary:

No one can understand ... unless one has seen the rows of dead men laid out. One sees men with their jaws blown off, arms and legs mutilated.

In August 1914, the town of Accrington was less worried about the war than that the town's biggest employer, Howard & Bullough's machine works, had locked out its workers for asking for a pay rise. An emotional appeal by Lady Louise Selina Maxwell for a pals' battalion to be raised was quickly filled. On the first day of the Battle of the Somme, 1 July 1916, the Accrington Pals, 700 strong, were sent into combat for the first time: 238 were killed immediately, and 350 wounded.

The Waterside in Derry, where many Ulster Volunteers were recruited, was particularly hard-hit. As the telegrams from the war office began to arrive women learned that they had lost fathers, sons, brothers, husbands and lovers; 'the women were out in the streets, screaming and crying', remembered James Conaghan: 'some homes had lost more than one man'. Also, the small town of Ballyclare had over thirty killed and more than one hundred wounded, so that 'for several weeks after the first of July, every time they heard a knock at the door their hearts nearly stopped beating'.[34]

When the Secretary of State for War, Lord Kitchener, asked Edward Carson at the start of the war, 'could you supply a Brigade of Ulster Volunteers, should England call?' Carson replied, 'I shall not supply a brigade, I will supply a Division'. In 1916 Kitchener fed that Division into the mincer.[35]

The 36th Ulster Division and the 16th Irish Division were more successful in 1917 at the Battle of Messines, where the 'ground was captured largely by the efforts of 30,000 Irishmen'. They lost just 2000 men that day. The German 2nd Division had been due for relief, but were packed tight together into Spanbroekmolen ready for a raid, and were caught when the British Army attacked first. Allied ammonal mines underneath German trenches at

**UVF-National Volunteer unity killed 20,000 Germans at
Messines Ridge**

Messines Ridge were detonated. 'They all went up in the air',
said Bob Grange. 'I never saw such carnage like it in such a short
space', he said. 'There wasn't a human body' intact, 'just bits and
pieces, arms, heads, feet, legs'.[36] All but ten men of the German
2nd Division of 10,000 were killed. Overall German losses were
20,000. In 1998 Fine Gael MP Paddy Harte and the Ulster Defence
Association's Glen Barr honoured the massacre as 'a symbolic
message that Irishmen from both north and south could join in a
common cause after the war'.[37]

Around seventeen million people died in the war, ten million
military and six million civilian deaths; a further twenty million
were wounded.

The growing revolt against the war

Though the beginning of the Great War silenced domestic
criticism, it only submerged those tensions – tensions between
labour and capital, between metropolitan countries and their

hinterlands, over relations between the sexes. Over time these tensions would re-emerge, only now they were exacerbated by all the strains that fighting the war had put upon society.

Dragooning millions of men from home town to training camp to battlefield, and then subjecting them to immense and deadly force, was in itself bound to provoke some reaction. Insubordination, absconding and outright mutinies were a constant challenge to military authority. Around 2000 men in the British Army were charged with mutiny between 1914 and 1922, and almost all of them found guilty. The greatest problems came at the end of the war, but already in 1915 there were a number of protests in training camps like that of the 152 Field Company Royal Engineers who refused to parade over poor food and accommodation, at Tidworth; in August 1916 at the Blargies Military Prison, hundreds of prisoners protested over oppressive treatment and refused to work, and two of them, Gunner William Lewis and New Zealander John Braithwaite, were executed for mutiny.

Perhaps the best-known insubordination was the Christmas truce, 1914, where 100,000 British and German troops stopped fighting, without official sanction. Soldiers from opposite sides met, exchanged gifts, sang across no-man's land to each other and according to legend played football. The truces were attacked by officers and eventually broken up. The following Christmas extra barrages were ordered to dissuade troops, though there were some haphazard acts of fraternisation all through the war.

At the Étaples base where troops were readied for the front, there was a concerted challenge to military authority in September 1917. There was an argument over a man being sent to the stockade for returning late from leave in the town. The following day, troops broke curfew and crossed over a bridge into the town of Étaples where they stayed out drinking. For the next few evenings the same challenge between officers and men took place, with the men overrunning armed pickets to leave the camp.

In Northern France in 1917 there were a number of mutinies in colonial labour units. South African Native Labour Corps men were court-martialled for striking in Dieppe in mid-March. Egyptian labour units had been involved in protests from May onwards. They were angry at the bullying officers and were kept segregated from white troops. On 23 July a man with the South African Native Labour Corps at No 7 camp in Dieppe was arrested for having defied an officer. When his fellow men used a pick-axe to free him and gathered in a crowd they were fired on by officers, killing four and wounding eleven; sixteen were tried and given field punishment. At Dunkirk on 22 May 1917, 1,925 men of the Egyptian Labour Corps secured increased rations when they threatened a strike.

In Britain, workplace strife had not been entirely abolished despite the Treasury Agreement. The militant engineers had been put to work in war industries, making guns and munitions. In Glasgow the conflict was most intense. In February 1915 9,000 engineers struck on Clydeside. They were trying to stop 'dilution', the substitution of skilled by unskilled labour – an issue that was potentially quite divisive – but done mostly to protect workers' interests and try to keep some control over the acceleration of production. In itself it was not a strike against the war, but the Clyde workers were resistant to the moral blackmail they got from the government and employers who were charging them with undermining the war effort. That was in large part down to the anti-war campaigning of some of the leading lights of the ad hoc Clyde Workers Committee, in particular John Maclean and Willie Gallacher, and more circumspectly Emmanuel Shinwell and Davy Kirkwood. When the Clyde Workers Committee organised 10,000 to protest and threaten a strike against rent rises, the government stepped in and ordered a rent freeze. On the other hand, they made sure that Maclean was imprisoned under the Defence of the Realm Act. In South

Wales 200,000 miners struck in defiance of the Munitions Act. In 1916 a National Shop Stewards Committee was organised to rally a rank and file defence of workers' interests.

After the collapse of the European Socialist Parties' anti-war plans, the radical opponents of war were beginning to put themselves together. Not just Maclean in Scotland, but the supporters of the Herald League in North London, were organising anti-war meetings. In East London, Sylvia Pankhurst broke with her sister to oppose the war, organising the East London Federation of Suffragettes, later renamed the Workers Socialist Federation. R. M. Fox of the North London Herald League got Davy Kirkwood down to speak at meetings in Finsbury Park about the Clyde Workers struggle; in East London Sylvia Pankhurst organised solidarity meetings too.

In Germany the socialists Karl Liebknecht and Friedrich Westermeyer coined the phrase, 'the main enemy is at home!' used in an anti-war leaflet in 1915. Liebknecht was isolated in the Reichstag, opposing the war. He was even called up, though in his sixties, and had to get special leave from his unit to speak at the sessions there. Later he would be imprisoned. With Rosa Luxemburg Liebknecht led a breakaway from the war-supporting Social Democrats that was called the Spartakusbund. Rosa Luxemburg wrote its pamphlets and newsletters, often from a prison cell.

There were strikes in Germany, too, in the face of the nationalist fury. One of the greatest clashes came when Karl Liebknecht was put on trial, and, on 28 June 1916, sentenced to two years and six months hard labour. When the trial began there were mass demonstrations in Berlin, and when the sentence was passed 55,000 munitions workers went on strike.

The Easter Rising

Early on in the war there were a number of attacks on British recruiting officers in Ireland. David Guiney, for example, was court-martialled for threatening officers of the Royal Munster Fusiliers in January 1915. Around the same time Irish Guards recruiting in Tralee were met by 'Sinn Feiners' marching through the town in opposition (Sinn Fein at that time was a small cultural nationalist group, sometimes used as a joint platform for wider layers of Irish nationalists, and the British habit of seeing their hand everywhere helped to push the organisation into a leading role). In December 1915 MP Thomas Kettle was barracked by as many as 200 republicans who demanded one of their own address the crowd – though afterwards the man was beaten to the ground by one of the soldiers present. A 'hostile mob of Sinn Feiners did their best to break' up a recruitment meeting in Killarney on 6 February 1916.[38]

The most audacious attack on recruitment though, was the infiltration and splitting of Redmond's Volunteers. From the outset the Irish Republican Brotherhood had set out to put itself at the heart of the Volunteers, for much the same reason that Redmond built them up in the first place. The Brotherhood thought that to carry weight, Ireland should carry arms. Where they broke with Redmond was in his commitment of the Volunteers to fight for the British Empire. Most of the Volunteers went with Redmond, but enough of a minority to count carried on as the Irish Volunteers, opposed to the British forces, including IRB men Tom Clarke Sean MacDermott, Joseph Plunkett and Thomas MacDonagh.

The Irish Volunteers' mustering and parading only led to one conclusion, and that was that they would take up arms to fight against the British Empire for Ireland. The rising was planned and put off and planned again. Alongside them in their protests against recruitment were often that other paramilitary group, James Connolly's Irish Citizens' Army. When conscription was brought in for Britain in January 1916 it seemed all too likely that it would be coming to Ireland, too. According to Seamus Reader, another motivation was the 'anti-conscription and the intended revolt on the Clyde' that 'did influence Countess Markiewicz, James Connolly and Sean MacDiarmid': 'They were determined that at least the Liffey would assert itself'.[39] That, and the greater threat of outright repression, was the reason that the Rising happened when it did. Connolly wrote:

> Free speech and a free press no longer exists. The Rights of Labour have been suppressed; to strike is an offence against the law whenever the authorities choose to declare it so; and all over these countries bands of soldiers and sailors are being encouraged to invade and break up meetings of civilians.
>
> Gradually the authorities have been making successful war upon every public right, gradually the mind of the unthinking has been accustomed to see without alarm the outraging of every constitutional liberty. That arbitrary exercise of power which two years ago would have evoked a storm of protest is now accepted with equanimity and even with approval.[40]

The Irish Volunteers' plans were at times confused, mostly because they were working partly in public, and partly underground – as they had to since their actions were all punishable under the Defence of the Realm Act. Ambiguity about whether they were just parading or setting out to conquer Ireland hampered their effectiveness, most pointedly in the confusion over the date of the rising. Eoin MacNeill was officially Chief of Staff, but the IRB men in the leadership of the Irish Volunteers made their plans without telling him, and presented him with a *fait accompli* a few days before it was to come off (originally Easter Sunday). MacNeill talked to those who were pushing for a Rising, and his account of their reasoning is put in the negative of his own argument that 'the only reason that could justify general active military measures on the part of the nationalists would be a reasonably calculated or estimated prospect of success'. He went on, in a direct rebuttal of the points that Connolly, Pearse and the others put to him, 'success in the operation itself, not merely some future moral or political advantage which may be hoped for as the result of non-success'.[41]

MacNeill's caution was understandable, but he was wrong to think the other side of the argument had abandoned military thinking in favour of idealism. Military theory has understood that moral force as well as material conditions were a factor since Clausewitz's *On War*, and Connolly in particular was familiar with Engel's reworking of Clausewitz, and had also made a point of publishing studies of the insurrections of 1830, 1848 and 1905 in the pages of the *Workers Republic*. Today few would doubt that a great deal of military actions can have propagandistic goals just as much as operational ones.

MacNeill sent out orders countermanding theirs, and confusion reigned. Most notably preparations for actions outside of Dublin did not come off, apart from those of Liam Mellows' 700 volunteers in County Galway.

Fighting in the streets of Dublin, 1916

For all the confusion, around 1500 Irish Volunteers and their comrades in the Irish Citizens' Army seized much of the centre of Dublin and held it against a British onslaught that shattered the city. After six days fighting they were beaten, and the remainder of them surrendered. From what we know there is little doubt that the leaders knew that they would lose, and most likely die – Connolly said so, and Pearse said that there would have to be a blood sacrifice for Ireland. This is a way of thinking that is pretty alien to today's postmodern bourgeois liberal for whom there is no cause worth dying for. But they could see Dublin emptying in front of them, and the lists of men killed at the front. The rising was not quixotic, but all too realistic.

The political leaders in Westminster did not take personal responsibility for what happened next, but kept command of the military repression at a distance, with plausible deniability for operational decisions. The Cabinet had told the Officer Commanding, General Maxwell, that it was at 'his discretion the dealing with particular cases, subject to the general instruction that death should not be inflicted except upon ringleaders'.[42] Later they would try to shift the blame onto the military for the executions. Of the 3,430 men and 79 women arrested, 90 were sentenced to death, and 16 were actually executed. 'In view of the gravity of the rebellion and its connection with German intrigue and propaganda', General Maxwell said, it was 'imperative to inflict the most severe sentences on the organisers of this detestable rising and on the commanders who took an actual part in the fighting which occurred'.[43] Countess Markiewicz was spared the firing squad as a woman – to her own protests; Éamon de Valera because he was at the back of the queue, and an American national.

The leaders of the uprising had hoped that their actions would stir a greater measure of support among the people. It has entered legend that the rebels were jeered by Dubliners when they were finally led away to jail by the British victors. No doubt some people did jeer, such as the wives of the soldiers serving in France, or the better-off supporters of Redmond's Irish Parliamentary Party. But there were reports, too, of crowds whose 'sympathies were with the rebels', and that 'there is a very menacing tone among the lower classes who openly praise the Sinn Feiners'.[44] The mood would change quite quickly as the British administration in Ireland looked more and more like a military occupation.

Mortar and cannon damage in Dublin, after the Rising

Chapter three

A shot that echoed around the world

It is often said of the assassination of the Archduke Ferdinand that it was a shot heard all around the world, but arguably the gunfire in Dublin had as great an impact. The Dubliners challenge shook the British Empire to its core, inspiring revolutionaries across the world. The Easter Rising was the first open rebellion against the war, followed by risings in Russia, Hungary and eventually Germany, which brought the slaughter to an end.[1]

British reaction

The most sustained reaction to the Easter Rising, of course, came from the British authorities that it most directly challenged. Not only had the rebels risen against the British Empire, but they had, as far as the British ruling class thought, stabbed them in the back as they were fighting for their lives against Germany. When James Connolly and Patrick Pearse were executed, even the liberal *Manchester Guardian* wrote: 'it is a fate which they invoked'.[2]

General Maxwell was the Commanding Officer of the British forces in Ireland. 'After I have finished with Dublin I propose to deal with the country', he said. Coercion became the norm. The political process stalled, as it became clear that John Redmond's support was ebbing away day by day, just as Sinn Fein's grew. Lloyd George tried to save Redmond with a deal, backed by the Unionist leaders Carson and Craig to hand authority for the south over to a Home Rule administration. The British elite rebelled, led by Lords Lansdowne, Balfour, Cromer, Halsbury, Midleton, Salisbury and Selborne. The Tory leader Lansdowne wrote on 28 June 1916, demanding to know 'whether under a Nationalist Government, Sir John Maxwell, with his 40,000 men, will be able to put down another Sinn Fein rebellion'. Do Messrs Redmond and Devlin, the Nationalist leaders,

> understand that if a Nationalist Government is set up, we shall still make use of the Defence of the Realm Acts, and that their suggestion that under the new dispensation the ordinary law will suffice cannot be entertained?[3]

And do they understand that 'Mr Devlin's promise of an immediate amnesty for the persons who are now imprisoned', Lansdowne added, 'cannot be entertained'? The next day the Tory and Unionist leaders rallied in the Carlton Club demanding firm measures and no compromise. The Unionists Carson and Craig backed off from the agreements he had made with Redmond and Lloyd George. A Royal Commission on the Rebellion concluded on 3 July that 'if the Irish system of Government be regarded as a whole it is anomalous in quiet times, and almost unworkable in times of crisis'. At the end of the month Asquith announced that the anomalous and unworkable system of rule from Westminster was to continue.

For the British elite the Irish unrest was as much of a test of British prestige as the war with Germany. 'If we lose Ireland we have lost the Empire', wrote Sir Henry Wilson.[4]

In March of 1918, Sir John French, Commander in Chief of the British Home Forces, was made Lord Lieutenant of Ireland, continuing the tradition of military rule. Lloyd George determined to impose conscription in Ireland. Éamon de Valera, having won a by-election in East Clare, led the opposition with a pledge:

> Denying the right of the British Government to enforce compulsory service in this country, we pledge ourselves solemnly to one another to resist Conscription by the most effective means at our disposal.

Sinn Fein then, far from being a militaristic organisation, was the most effective anti-war campaign in the United Kingdom. In support of the anti-conscription campaign an All-Ireland Labour Committee organised a general strike on 23 April 1918 – the first successful labour action against the war. In a manifesto the Irish Trade Union Congress called on workers in other countries to follow Ireland's example and 'rise up against their oppressors and bring the war to an end'.[5] The attempt to enforce conscription was foiled.

On 17 May French, with the approval of the cabinet, had the homes of the Sinn Fein leaders raided and took them into custody under the Defence of the Realm Act. It was his 'firm conviction that Ireland should be put at once under complete martial law'. At the end of July French proscribed the Irish Volunteers, Sinn Fein, Cumann na nBan (the women's organisation) and the Gaelic League as dangerous associations; he also proscribed public meetings and fairs under clause 9AA of the Defence of the Realm Act.[6]

On 14 December 1918, after the German surrender, Britain and Ireland went to the polls in the initial glow of victory. 'War has always been fatal to liberalism', Lloyd George acknowledged: 'Victory is the triumph of force and not of reason'. More, 'after every great war there is a period during which the belligerent nations incline to divide into two extreme camps – roughly known as revolutionary and reactionary'. The Conservative Party was triumphant, while the Liberals were divided between supporters and opponents of coalition. Labour did better, but the real upset was in Ireland. Sinn Fein put up candidates across Ireland, winning 73 seats. Many of their candidates were prisoners. The Irish Parliamentary Party was wiped out, and the Unionists, with 25 per cent of the vote, won 22 seats in the north east.

'There are only two parties in Ireland', editorialised the *Nottingham Evening Post*, 'loyal and disloyal'. The policy of Sinn

Fein is 'by any and every means to make mischief for Great Britain', added the Daily Telegraph, demanding of the government to 'take such steps as will make life and property secure', as 'there can be little doubt … a reign of terrorism will be attempted'. The reign of terrorism, though would come from the British authorities. Sinn Fein's offices in Dublin were raided, and the hall in Roscommon where the new MP Harry Boland was to give a lecture was occupied by police and soldiers to stop it.[7]

In April of 1919 British troops seized control of the city of Limerick. Citizens who wanted to pass in and out had to have a military-issued pass. In protest the Limerick Trades Council organised a General Strike across the city. Taking over the town the Trades Council even issued their own currency, and its assembly was called the Limerick Soviet by the foreign press.[8]

'Force is the only power that will solve the Irish question', Sir John French told Churchill. To Brigadier General Toby Long, French wrote on 1 July 1920:

We should take up the war-like challenge which the Sinn Feiners have sent us and declare war against them. With fifty or sixty thousand British troops, reinforced by Ulster volunteers, I think there is no doubt as to the result.[9]

In August 1920 the Restoration of Order in Ireland Act was passed giving French special powers for a crackdown. The First Lord of the Admiralty Sir Walter Long had written to French saying he should use the demobilised servicemen to shore up the Royal Irish Constabulary. In June 1920 the Ministry of Labour reported that there were 167,000 ex-servicemen on unemployment benefits. Ex-servicemen were recruited into the RIC – more than 10,000 of them between 1920 and 1921. The RIC's Inspector General Joseph Byrne was alarmed, or as Long wrote to French, he 'had lost his nerve', and was replaced. Known as the 'Black and Tans' because of their makeshift uniforms, part RIC, part army surplus, the force were also known for hundreds of atrocities all over Ireland. Their first action, after an RIC head constable was shot in Balbriggan on 20 September 1920, was to raid the town that night, killing two men, looting and burning four public houses, destroying a hosiery factory, and damaging or destroying 49 private homes. When the attack was criticised in the English press, recruitment shot up. 'When we begin to act we must act like a sledgehammer, so as to cause bewilderment and consternation among the people of southern Ireland', said Churchill.[10]

Ireland under occupation, 1920

Despite the 40,000-strong force of British troops, RIC, Black and Tans and Ulster Special Constabulary French could not stop the Sinn Fein MPs from making themselves up into an Irish Parliament, the Dáil, and with the war at a stalemate, peace talks were opened. The British proposal, a Treaty, was well calculated to divide the moderate and militant republicans, offering self-government in the south, but with the loss of the north east, and with an oath of allegiance to the British Crown. After agonising debates the two sides could not agree: IRA Commander Michael Collin, Arthur Griffith, W. T. Cosgrave and Kevin O'Higgins narrowly won the vote to accept the Treaty; de Valera, Erskine Childers, Mary MacSwiney, Constance Markiewicz and Rory O'Connor opposed. The Indian MP for Battersea Saklatvala charged that the House of Commons pretended it was 'giving this Irish Treaty with a view to bringing peace to Ireland, but we know that it is not bringing peace'. Further, he said that 'as in 1801 England gave them a forced Union, so in 1922 England is giving them a forced freedom'.

Divided against themselves, the Irish challenge to British might could at least be contained if it could not be overturned. In 1922 the anti-Treaty IRA ambushed and killed Henry Wilson, wartime hero to the British, 'Orange terror' to the Irish. Churchill pressed the pro-Treaty government to take action against the IRA, which they did, bombarding their headquarters in the Four Courts, with British-loaned eighteen pounders. Anti-treaty republicans Rory O'Connor, Liam Mellows and many more were killed in the fighting, Erskine Childers executed for carrying arms. The pro-Treaty forces suffered, too, when Michael Collins was killed in an ambush, and Arthur Griffith died of a stroke, leaving W. T. Cosgrave to impose an armed and paranoid peace. Not at that time an Irish Republic, but *An Saorstat*, the 'Free State' in the south, Ireland denuded of its industrial base in the northern Six Counties, in the country of Ulster, which were created what its leader Viscount Craigavon would call 'a Protestant State for a Protestant people'. In final settlement talks with Cosgrave in 1925, the British even got the Free State to pay £1,500,000 a year in 'land annuities' for the grants made under the land reform of the 1880s.

Even after succeeding in plunging Ireland into a Civil War, Britain's leaders were in shock at the blow they had received in Easter 1916. In 1933 commemoration of the Rising had been banned by the Ulster Minister of Home Affairs under the Civil Authorities (Special Powers) Act. All the same, 'over 5000 people knelt in prayer under the observation of police with drawn batons near Milltown Cemetery, Belfast' (*Dundee Evening Telegraph*, 17 April 1933). The following year 'police were on duty at the cemetery from midnight and at Roman Catholic churches from early morning, as well as at other points, to prevent an organised demonstration' in Derry, though a meeting was held in the street and the proclamation read. In 1940 the Governor of Dartmoor jail imposed a lock-down to stop prisoners' plans to commemorate the Rising, complaining of 'a large number of IRA terrorists being detained in the same jail'.[11]

The British Cabinet were at first surprised, and then scandalised, that in 1932 Éamon de Valera's new Fianna Fail party won the elections in the Free State, repudiating the Treaty. It was, said, Churchill in Plymouth on 17 March 1932, an 'act of perfidy', adding that if Mr de Valera and his Government repudiate the Treaty 'they repudiate the title deeds of the Irish Free State, which becomes an anomalous body without status at all, either in or out of the Empire'. De Valera also repudiated the land annuities that Cosgrave had agreed to pay, and put tariffs on English goods. This was the first shot in an 'economic war' that carried on until 1938. Civil Servants complained that 'there is no room for compromise about the land annuities' – as if the British Empire would crumble without this backdoor exploitation of Irish farmers. On the other hand they wanted to avoid arbitration since they knew that the informal agreement between Cosgrave and Lloyd George had not been ratified by the Dáil, so their legal case was weak. In retaliation, Britain raised tariffs against Irish goods. The *Manchester Guardian* blamed the 'fanaticism of de Valera' for the trouble. After de Valera won a second election, the Cabinet softened its stance and negotiated a restoration of trade.[12]

In 1939 Churchill wanted to take back Ireland's ports by force

Britain was again roused to anger at de Valera's government in the Second World War, as the Taoiseach (Prime Minister) kept Ireland neutral. Winston Churchill wanted control of Ireland's strategic ports, Berehaven (Castletown) and Queenstown (Cobh), and advised the admiralty that 'if the U-boat campaign becomes more effective we should coerce southern Ireland about coast watching and about Berehaven etc'. There was anger in the British cabinet, too, that Ireland was not sharing the burden of austerity. De Valera offered to join the war if the British would talk to Craigavon and the Unionists about joining an all-Ireland government, but Churchill blocked an agreement. Lord Cranborne thought that among answers to the problem 'the first and most obvious was to march in, horse, foot and artillery', and occupy the country, but failing that they could again impose economic sanctions. [13]

Trying to explain their hatred of the men and women of Easter 1916 the British elite tied themselves in knots. At the time many claimed that the Rising was a German plot – an allegation that is still made today – and Conservative and Unionist MPs in the House of Commons would demand an investigation into the

German links to Sinn Fein. But just as often it would be alleged that Sinn Fein was a Bolshevik conspiracy. The *Spectator*'s response to the 1918 election sweep was that 'the end will be that Sinn Fein will take on a Bolshevik character, and will prove to be the means by which a great many of the Irish people will be drawn into heresy and the renunciation of all religious ties and duties'.[14]

The mainstream, elite reaction to the Easter Rising and its aftermath, however, was not the only one in Britain.

Radical reaction in Britain

The impact of the Easter Rising worldwide has rarely been acknowledged. The Great War that begun in 1914 threw all progress into reverse, not just in its sacrifice of millions of men and women, but also in the succour it gave to reaction. Britain as well as Ireland was under military rule and 'national government', with forced labour under the munitions act, and the end of freedom to speak or organise under the Defence of the Realm Act. Militarist propaganda poisoned the country, encouraging reactionaries to attack anyone who questioned the war effort.

There had been strikes and even some mutinies, but the Easter Rising was the first real revolution against the war effort. All those who wanted to stop the war were lifted by the blow that Dublin struck against the Empire. Eighteen-year-old Patricia Lynch who campaigned against the war with both the North London Herald Club and the East London Socialist Federation bought a ticket and went to Dublin, and wrote vivid reports of the repression for the *Workers' Dreadnought*. Sylvia Pankhurst's editorial ran alongside Lynch's articles, saying 'Justice can make but one reply to the Irish rebellion, and that is to demand that Ireland should be allowed to govern herself'. Pankhurst warned that 'the "firm and vigorous" administration which the *Times* demands for Ireland' would be 'but another term for coercion'.

In her diaries Pankhurst noted the 'amazing doings' in Dublin, and how 'the little Republic of a week' was promising 'equal rights and opportunities' for all citizens: 'Amid the destruction and the carnage shone the fire of idealism and bravery'. That her friends and allies in the struggle for women's rights, Maud Gonne, Constance Markiewicz, Charlotte Despard and the murdered Francis Sheehy-Skeffington were all active in the struggle for Irish freedom no doubt confirmed her response. She said:

I knew that the Easter Monday rebellion was the first blow in an intensified struggle, which would end in Irish self-government. I knew that the execution of the rebels had irrev- ocably ensured the ultimate success of their uprising.

The *Workers Dreadnought* articles were reprinted as a pamphlet *Rebel Ireland*, which sold well among the growing number of workers in Britain who were turning against the War.

Patricia Lynch was not the only Londoner who went to Dublin. Joe Good got there in time to join the rebels in the GPO, and later wrote a memoir of the Rising. Glaswegians Denis Canning, Liam Gribben and Patrick James McGuire also joined the uprising, and are honoured today in Scotland. Volunteers went from Liverpool, too, to fight for Ireland's freedom.

Countess Constance Markiewicz was the first woman to win a seat in a Westminster election, but sat instead in Dáil Eireann

The *Daily Herald*, the popular left-wing paper, carried an appreciation of Connolly by Desmond Ryan, who had fought in the Rising:

> Loathing the present war, and consistently with the teachings of a lifetime which identified political independence with social freedom, he rose and fought and died.

Ryan felt he had to argue Connolly's case against socialist critics who did not understand the commitment to national liberation:

> Well will it be for his critics if they can show something of his dauntless adherence to principle and much of his iron soul! Equally helpful will it be for his critics, if they remember the circumstances in which he worked and his forty-six years of noble and strenuous service to the fighters against the dominion of nation over nation, of class over class, of sex over sex.

The background to the Easter Rising, argued Ryan, was the failure of the socialists to challenge the war:

> For the world in general, too frequently the trumpets of war sound a farewell to those battles. With James Connolly it was not so, and he began at home.[15]

In Leeds, Tom Jackson had kept up a vociferous campaign against the war with his local branch of the Independent Labour Party. He had met James Connolly in 1913 through a friend in common Con Lyhane. When he got the news of Connolly's execution he organised an emergency meeting of support in the Leeds Town Hall. Jackson kept up the solidarity work for Ireland, staying there in 1920 to report on it for the socialist press, and in 1947 he wrote and published a fine history *Ireland Her Own*, where he makes a strong case for the Rising.

In Glasgow the socialist leader John MacLean took pride in the news that Connolly had taken heart for his venture from the struggles of the Clyde side workers. Maclean threw himself into solidarity work for the nascent Irish Republic. In 1920 he toured scores of towns in Scotland on a speaking tour, asking workers to 'strike, then, for the withdrawal of British troops from Ireland'. 'Britain's retention of Ireland is the world's most startling instance of a "dictatorship by terrorists"', said Maclean, in a pamphlet, *The Irish Tragedy*, of which 20,000 copies were sold: 'Britain rules Ireland against Irish wishes with policemen armed with bombs and a huge army'.[16]

Industrial action against British repression in Ireland was not a pious dream. The idea came from the leader of the young Soviet Republic in Russia, Lenin. Grateful for the solidarity action that the British workers had taken blacking the export of war material to be used against the Soviet Union, Karl Radek counselled that it would be harder, but better, if British comrades 'take up the cause of Irish independence'; 'it is their duty to use all their resources to block the policy that the British transport and railway unions are at present pursuing of permitting troop transports to be shipped to Ireland', he said. The Russian Revolution had inspired a new party in Britain, and among its first commitments was this: 'The news that comes daily from Ireland is in itself a summons to the Communist Party of Great Britain', and 'Not only the Irish, but the working class all the world over is looking to us'. So it was that the '"Hands off Russia" movement was supplemented by a "Hands off Ireland" movement' on the docks and railways in the summer of 1920.[17]

While the anti-war socialists took up the cause of Ireland, the pro-war Labour Party leaders were violently against it. The National Union of Railways leader Jimmy Thomas had fought against Jim Larkin's influence with Irishmen in his union in 1913, and in 1920 he stamped down hard on the 'Hands off Ireland' solidarity actions. Even the Glasgow paper *Forward* objected that 'a man must either be a nationalist or an internationalist'. But Arthur MacManus' Communist Party countered that in 'the case of a small nation held in forcible suppression by a great imperialist state the national struggle and the class struggle are inseparable from one another.'[18]

Belfast erupts

The most remarkable of all the blows against Britain's war in industry took place in Belfast, in January and February of 1919, just as the Dáil Eireann was sitting in Dublin. Engineers and shipbuilders led a general strike of 40,000, mostly Protestant, workers that gripped the city for two weeks. The workers' Strike Bulletin demanded the 53-hour week they were working be cut to 44 to make up for the 'four long years' – the war – over which they 'endured the grind of inhuman hours under the spur of necessity. The strikers drew on, and subverted the discipline and organisation of the Ulster Covenant. The strike committee's Harry Howard parodied Randolph Churchill's anti-Home Rule speech of 1886, saying: 'Labour will fight and labour will be right. Labour can stand alone!'

The loyalist press and politicians denounced the strikers. 'The forces which control Sinn Fein and organised labour are marching hand in hand on the lines of approved Bolshevism', said the Irish Unionist Alliance; 'Sinn Fein tricked out as Labour with its red flag', editorialised the *Belfast Newsletter*; the strike committee were 'practically Sinn Feiners', said Sir James Craig. The Irish Trade Union Congress did lend support to the Belfast strikes, but the strikers' allegiance to Sinn Fein only existed in the minds of their fear-struck Orange overlords.[19] In the end the strike was broken by the use of British troops on 15 February, proving that loyalty only ran in one direction.

Well might the people of the northern Six Counties of Ulster rebel against the cost of the war, run ragged in the factories, bearing 32,000 casualties among the Ulster Volunteer Force. Edward Carson, who had dragooned those men to their deaths, and offered up the industrial sacrifice, tried to redirect anger at the Dublin-based Republic, and at Catholics in the north of Ireland. In a speech on 12 July 1920 he called on the Ulster Volunteers to reorganise against the threat of 'Sinn Fein'. The speech triggered a race war against Catholics that terrorised them out of the factories. 7,500 men and women were victims of the industrial expulsions. Catholics were attacked in the streets over three nights of rioting. Among those expelled was James Baird of the strike committee of 1919. Another was John Hanna, who had been an Orange Lodge leader. He said:

> During the strike for 44-hrs week the capitalist classes saw that the Belfast workers were one. That unity had to be broken, it was accomplished by appeals to the basest passions and intense bigotry.

Strike leader Sam Kyle thought the Belfast strike 'gave the biggest scare to the Tories they ever had, and probably led to the engineering pogrom of 1920'.[20]

Relief Committees for the expelled were set up in the south, amongst the Irish world-wide, and in Britain. The independence of the Belfast labour movement was shattered. On this sectarian foundation the Government of Northern Ireland was built the following year.

Revolt against the war breaks through

Should the working class of Europe, rather than slaughter each other for the benefit of kings and financiers, proceed tomorrow to erect barricades all over Europe, to break up bridges and destroy the transport service that war might be abolished, we should be perfectly justified in following such a glorious example and contributing our aid to the final dethronement of the vulture classes that rule and rob the world...

Starting thus, Ireland may yet set the torch to a European conflagration that will not burn out until the last throne and the last capitalist bond and debenture will be shrivelled on the last pyre of the last warlord.

–James Connolly, *Irish Worker*, 8 August 1914

James Connolly's hopes for a revolution against the war in 1914 were just too soon. Europe's statesmen and crowned heads had outmanoeuvred the socialists, by stirring a national sentiment among a much wider body of the unorganised masses, and largely silenced them – but at great cost. Waging war put great pressure on all nations, which strained at the seams. The Easter Rising was the first open revolt against Europe's warlords. Though it was crushed, it would set the torch to a European conflagration.

James Connolly's son Roddy with Lenin in 1921

In May 1916 an article, 'Their song is over', was published in a socialist newspaper the *Berner Tagwacht*, which dismissed the Easter Rising as a 'putsch'. The Russian socialist V. I. Lenin, wrote a stinging rebuke to the author:

To imagine that social revolution is conceivable without revolts by small nations in the colonies and in Europe, without revolutionary outbursts by a section of the petty bourgeoisie with all its prejudices, without a movement of the politically non-conscious proletarian and semi-proletarian masses against oppression by the landowners, the church, and the monarchy, against national oppression, etc. – to imagine all this is to repudiate social revolution. So one army lines up in one place and says, "We are for socialism", and another, somewhere else and says, "We are for imperialism", and that will be a social revolution! Only those who hold such a ridiculously pedantic view could vilify the Irish rebellion by calling it a "putsch".

Lenin added:

Whoever expects a "pure" social revolution will never live to see it. Such a person pays lip-service to revolution without understanding what revolution is. (October 1916 in *Sbornik Sotsial-Demokrata* No. 1)

Lenin welcomed the 'blow delivered against the power of the English imperialist bourgeoisie by a rebellion in Ireland'. It was, he argued, the first step in the European revolution.

Four months after this article, nine months after the Easter Rising, the people of Russia revolted against their Tsar and put the liberal Kerensky in power; nine months after that, it becoming clear that Kerensky still wanted to commit Russia to the slaughter on the Eastern Front, a second revolution founded

the Soviet Union, with Lenin's Bolsheviks as its effective leaders.
The example of Easter 1916 rang around the world. The
Trinidadian revolutionary C.L.R. James wrote that it was 'the first
blow struck against imperialism during the war at a time when
the revolutionary movement in Europe seemed sunk in apathy'.
Shortly after the Soviet revolution in Russia took up arms to take
the nation out of the war. Then the Hungarian revolution led by
Bela Kun did the same. In 1919 Egypt revolted against the British
rule, while in India the British opening fire on a protest at the
Jallianwalla Bagh at Amritsar led to hundreds of deaths, and
scores of protests against British rule. Leon Trotsky wrote that

> the British Socialist who fails to support by all possible means
> the uprisings in Ireland, Egypt and India against the London
> plutocracy – such a Socialist deserves to be branded with
> infamy, if not with a bullet.[21]

The Kiel Mutiny

In the 100th anniversary of the opening of the Great War, the
Channel 4 journalist Paul Mason put forward the question that
seemed to have escaped most looking back: 'How did the First

World War actually end?' The answer is that in October 1918, hearing that they were to be sent on a desperate sortie, sailors in the ports of Hamburg, Kiel, Wilhelmshaven revolted. They seized the ports, and then went in their thousands to the main cities, like Bremen and Berlin, to demand an end to the war. The German revolution of 1918 won the abdication of the Kaiser on 9 November, and the war ended two days later. Paul Mason explains that the socialist underground had been building up its organisation in the northern ports since Easter 1916.[22]

In February 1919 delegates of the Irish Trades Union Congress were greeted at the meeting of the Socialist International conference at Berne. In April the follow up conference in Amsterdam the International called on the Peace Conference to 'make good this rightful claim of the Irish people'.[23]

The Easter Rising in the British Army

'For me it began in far-off Mesopotamia, now called Iraq', recalled Tom Barry who had joined the British Army at the age of seventeen, in Cork, 1915. 'I cannot plead I went on the advice of John Redmond', he wrote, saying that he had no higher calling than that he 'wanted to see what war was like, get a gun, to see new countries and feel a man'. Barry was looking at a notice-board where the war news was put up, and read there: 'REBELLION IN DUBLIN' – 'it told of the shelling of the Dublin GPO and Liberty Hall and of hundreds of rebels killed, thousands arrested and leaders being executed'. 'It was a rude awakening', wrote Barry, 'guns being fired at the people of my own race by soldiers of the same army that I was serving'.[24]

Tom Barry returned to Ireland at the end of the war, and promptly put his warrior's training to work fighting against the British Army. As Commander of the West Cork Flying Column of the Irish Republican Army, Barry harassed and pinned down British forces of 12,500 men.

In 1922, Sir Henry Wilson, former Chief of the General

Imperial Staff, had taken up politics as the Member of Parliament for North Down, in which role he championed stern measures against the south. On 22 June he was ambushed in Liverpool Street Stations by two IRA men, Reginald Dunne and Joseph O'Sullivan. Both had served in Wilson's army, Dunne as a private on the Western Front with the Irish Guards, O'Sullivan as a Lance Corporal. At trial, they agreed that Dunne should read a statement:

> We both joined voluntarily for the purpose of taking human life, in order that the principles for which this country stood should be upheld and preserved. Those principles we were told were self-determination and freedom for small nations.
>
> We came back from France to find that Self Determination had been given to some nations we had never heard of, but that it had been denied Ireland.[25]

In 1920 a company of the Connaught Rangers were stationed at the Wellington Barracks in Jullundur, India. They could not be stationed in Ireland, because those regiments that were largely Irish were not trusted there.[26] On 28 June they refused to work as a protest against the British Army's action in Ireland 'where they consider their friends are being oppressed'. On hearing about the protest at Jullundur another company of Connaught Rangers at Solon also rebelled. Sixty-nine men were tried for mutiny, fourteen were at the time sentenced to death by firing squad – though all but one of the sentences were commuted to life imprisonment. Private James Daly was executed in Dagshai Prison, 2 November 1920.

The Secretary of State telegrammed the Viceroy of India on 9 July 1920:

> We have every reason to believe that the whole affair was engineered by Sinn Fein. Large Sinn Fein flags were hoisted in

the barracks when the mutiny broke out at Jullundur ... Sinn Fein colours and rosettes were also worn.

The soldiers explained themselves by saying, 'if you were to be shot, stick up for your Irish home which is ruined by the troops in our dear country'. 'It is our duty to fight now and make her free once more', they wrote on a placard. 'Look at what they done, 1916', said another. When the men began their mutiny, the re-named their barracks Liberty Hall after the headquarters of the Irish Citizen's Army.

Army mutinies after the armistice

The Connaught Rangers mutiny stood out as a direct and political revolt in the army over the British repression in Ireland, with a clear goal of liberation. Mutiny in the British Army at that time, however, was not uncommon. There were mutinies all through 1919 on the part of men who were determined to go home. Historian Julian Putkowski says that 'in late January and early February there was hardly a major camp in Britain unaffected by strikes and mass demonstrations or protest marches'. 'The trouble began', he says, 'at Dover and Folkestone on 3 January when 9–10,000 soldiers returning to the continent after Christmas leave refused to embark on the ferries'. In time 'direct action was taken by no fewer than 50,000 more soldiers, all demanding accelerated demobilisation'. Only three men were charged with mutiny, as the military authorities and government tried to avoid a fight. Sir Basil Thompson, the Special Branch Metropolitan Police Commissioner, said that 'during the first three months of 1919 unrest touched its high watermark', and 'I do not think at any time in history since the Bristol Riots we have been so near to revolution'.[27]

Alongside the Bolshevik Revolution in Russia, the German revolution and the abdication of the Kaiser, the Uprising and the Tan War in Ireland, these mutinies and attacks on authority

**British, American, Canadian and Australian troops took on the
Metropolitan Police in the 'Battle of Bow Street', 1919**

made up a wave of protest across Europe. Lloyd George wrote
this memo to Clemenceau outlining the problem:

The whole of Europe is filled with the spirit of revolution.
There is a deep sense not only of discontent but of anger and
revolt amongst the workmen against the pre-war conditions. The
whole existing order in its political, social and economic aspects
is questioned by the masses of the population from one end of
Europe to the other.[28]

The imprisoned Connaught Rangers, even those whose
sentences had been commuted to life imprisonment, were
released, at Churchill's request, in the hope of securing a
settlement in the talks that would lead to the Anglo-Irish Treaty
of 1921. The men – apart from James Daly – returned home to a
hero's welcome. The War of Independence was not an isolated
act, but the end of a cycle of uprising, mutinies, and revolutions
that began in Dublin, found an even greater echo in Moscow and
St Petersburg in 1917, and was taken up in the German revolution
that ended the war and in the soldiers' mutinies that forced

demobilisation. As well as signalling the beginning of the end of the Great War, the Easter Rising would echo further throughout the British Empire in the years afterwards.

The Easter Rising and the British Empire

Not since British Kaffraria was handed back to its native people in 1837 had the British Empire retreated, let alone been overthrown, and that was reversed after ten years. The victory of the war of liberation (however incomplete) was a blow at British prestige that was watched carefully throughout the Empire, and by colonised peoples across the world.

India's emerging national movement, in particular, was electrified by the republicans' success in freeing themselves from the British yoke – as excellently researched and set out by historian Michael Silvestri.[29] 'Bravo!' the Indian paper *Ghadr* saluted the Easter Rising: 'O Irish, you kept your sword on high and did not show the white feather' (19 August 1917). In 1920 Dáil Eireann sent Art O'Brien and Sean T. O'Kelly to London to talk to Indian revolutionaries who wanted help, and the following year more meetings took place in Berlin and Moscow between Irish and Indian nationalists, brokered by the Communist Party of the Soviet Union.

In February 1919 Lajpat Rai told the Irish Race Convention in Philadelphia that by 1925 there would be more Sinn Feiners in India than in Ireland. The following year the Friends of Freedom in India joined the St Patrick's Day Parade in New York wearing turbans of gold and green, led by Sailendranath Ghose on a horse. They published a leaflet:

Help India to liberty and independence. The British Empire can alone be destroyed by separating India from it. Only INDEPENDENT INDIA can save America, Ireland, Egypt and the whole world from the BRITISH PERIL.

The Friends of Freedom for India called the Easter Rising 'Ireland's Amritsar' and predicted of the perpetrator of the Amritsar Massacre: 'we may expect soon to hear of General Dyer's being assigned to duty in Ireland' (newsletter, 29 May 1920). Éamon de Valera gave a speech at a rally they held saying that 'we of Ireland and you of India, must both of us endeavour, both as separate peoples and in combination, to rid ourselves of the vampire that is fattening on our blood'. As the setting was America, he added, 'we must never forget to what weapon it was by which Washington rid his country of this same vampire', and 'our cause is a common cause'. The speech was printed over the front page of the *Irish World* of 6 March 1920 – which was banned from import to India.

The British India Government was set to keep any rebels out. The Viceroy said that no passports should be given to 'Bolshevists, Sinn Feiners, members of the International Workers of the World, or Revolutionary Party in Egypt' (7 January 1920).

The rising challenge to British rule in Bengal in particular took heart from the Irish example, so that Nirad Chaudhuri teased the revolutionaries that they 'thought they were the Sinn Fein of India'. Calcutta Police Commissioner J. H. Colson sent an urgent report about a pamphlet put out by the United Socialist Republican Party 'with portraits side-by-side of Subhas Chandra Bose ... and the late Michael Collins, the head of the IRA'. The headline read 'What Ireland has done Bengal will do' (28 June 1934).

The Indian nationalist Bose visited Ireland, meeting on many occasions with Éamon de Valera, as well as Sean Lemass, and the anti-Treatyites Mary MacSwiney, Maud Gonne Macbride and Hannah Sheehy Skeffington. 'India as a whole has been influenced by Ireland's fight for independence', Bose claimed, and told a friend that where he was from 'there is hardly an educated family where books about the Irish heroes are not read' or even 'devoured'.

In 1929 the police found a leaflet urging young Bengalis to 'read and learn the history of Pearse – the gem of young Ireland, and you will find how noble is his sacrifice': 'Pearse died and by so dying he roused in the heart of the nation an indomitable desire for armed revolution'. Indians honoured other Irish heroes, including Terence MacSwiney who 'was almost worshipped by politically conscious Bengalis', according to Nirad Chaudhuri, and the Mayor of Calcutta sent a message of condolence to his widow, saying that he 'showed the way to Ireland's freedom', as well as inspiring Indians. Connaught Ranger mutineer James Daly's grave in Jullundur also became a shrine for Indian nationalists.

Dan Breen's *My Fight for Irish Freedom* was translated into Hindi, Punjabi, Tamil and Burmese – and every edition was banned

Dan Breen's memoir *My Fight for Irish Freedom* was published in no less than four different languages in the British Empire in the East, Hindi, Punjabi, Tamil and Burmese – and each one was banned by the colonial authorities. It was, said Chinmohan Sehnabis, 'one of our bibles'.

In 1930 a battalion of Bengali nationalists attempted a revolution, storming government offices in Chittagong, but were overpowered. At their trial the Chittagong District Magistrate H.R. Wilkinson said that Breen's book 'might aptly be described as the Revolutionaries' Manual' and said that the group were 'thoroughly conversant with it'. 'Dan Breen's book is held up as a text book for the revolutionaries of India', claimed Wilkinson; 'the action of the revolutionaries was largely inspired by this book and their plan of operations was based upon its lessons' (10 October 1930).

The Director of the Intelligence Bureau of India agreed, thinking that 'the comparative success of the methods adopted by the Irish terrorists from 1916 to 1922 had stirred the imagination of the revolutionaries, and there is no doubt that the latter's tactics have been closely modelled on those of the Sinn Feiners'. He thought it was significant that 'like the Irish insurrection in Dublin in 1916, the raid took place at Easter'.

Beyond India

In Burma in 1937 Ba Maw and Aung San – who would both govern the country after the war – set up the National Revolutionary Party on the model of the Irish Republican Party to take advantage of Britain's difficulties with the Japanese in the Far East. The Burmese nationalists had a ready stock of Sinn Fein propaganda – including the Burmese translation of Dan Breen's book – available from a radical bookshop in Rangoon, run by J.S. Furnivall.[30]

The young Ho Chi Minh, before he was President of Vietnam, travelled around Europe and America between 1912 and 1919 stopping in London and Paris, working as a cook and a dishwasher in London. 'He saw how England, the largest colonial Empire in the world, harshly suppressed Ireland's quest for independence', reports his biographer Pierre Brocheux, and was particularly impressed that the Irish took up arms in 1916 'right in the middle of World War I'. He wrote in his diary that he cried when he heard of the death of MacSwiney, saying 'a nation which has such citizens will never surrender'.[31]

Nine years later Ho met up with representatives of the Irish Republican Army Sean MacBride and Peader O'Donnell under the banner of the Congress of the League Against Imperialism in Frankfurt, along with the Indian nationalists Chato Padaya and Pandit Nehru. The fledgling Soviet Union that sponsored the meeting was the first country to offer to recognise the independent Irish republic, in 1921, but de Valera, worried that it would offend America, asked them not to announce it. [32]

Sean MacBride was son to John MacBride who was executed in the Rising, and the boy went on to be Chief of Staff of the IRA, and then later Ireland's minister of Foreign Affairs, and also a renowned international jurist. Though he was officially no longer in the IRA, he was a fellow traveller who represented them in negotiations in 1976, and defended their members in court. As the United Nations Commissioner responsible he helped the South West Africa People's Organisation in its fight for freedom, earning the praise of its leader (and later President of Namibia) Sam Nujoma: 'he always took the right course'.[33]

At his funeral in Dublin in 1988, African National Congress leader Oliver Tambo said: 'We in the ANC have rich memories of a great Irishman, a revolutionary and freedom fighter, who recognised that freedom, like peace, was indivisible'. Kader Asmal, another ANC leader, was inspired by his father's stories of the Easter Rising. Asmal explained that where the ANC's Freedom Charter of 1955 set out that South Africa belongs to all who live in it, black and white, they drew on the Proclamation of

1916, and its declaration that all the children of the nation should be cherished equally. Asmal also fixed up for the IRA to help train the ANC's military wing at a camp in Luanda, in 1980, to great effect.[34]

Africans in America were inspired by the Easter Rising. The Jamaica-born leader of the United Negro Improvement Association, Marcus Garvey, was moved by the support that Éamon de Valera got when he arrived in America, and called the Association's building in Harlem, Liberty Hall. In a speech dedicating it he sang the praises of Robert Emmett and Roger Casement. When Terence MacSwiney died Irish-American dock workers struck out the ports, over August and September 1920. Garvey's supporters went to speak for the strikers, to make sure that black dock-workers joined the action. Another group, the African Blood Brotherhood, based in New York, hoped to build 'a great Pan-African army in the same way as the Sinn Fein built up the Irish Army under the very nose of England'.[35]

At the same time as the Irish War of Independence another great struggle for freedom was underway in Egypt. The Wafd Party had risen to prominence in a wave of protests and strikes, triggered by the expulsion of the popular leader Saad Zaghlul. Crowds shouted 'Long live Saad! Long live independence!' To try to calm the storm the British brought a delegation led by Prime Minister Adli Pasha around the same time that they were trying to negotiate a cessation of hostilities with the Sinn Fein leaders. To Churchill the Wafd and Sinn Fein were the same challenge, or, as the *Irish Times* put it, 'the Wafdists are the Sinn Fein party of Egypt'.[36]

Britain was also open to challenge in those parts of the world settled by Irish emigrants. Australians of Irish descent had been solidly for Home Rule, and so were initially alarmed by the Rising. Easter 1916 divided their loyalties between the Empire and Ireland, and the church was largely hostile to the rebels. As the news of the executions came through, though, public support for Britain soured, and Cardinal Daniel Mannix and *Catholic Press* editor John Tighe Ryan led protests against the repression there. Premier William Hughes tried to win the country to conscription with a referendum in December 1916, but lost, by his own account because of opposition from pacifists and the Irish. The Labour Party split over the conscription question, with many Irish supporters staying with the anti-conscription party as the pro-conscription group left. Another referendum for conscription was defeated the following year. In 1921 much of the country's political establishment went to the Irish Race Convention in Melbourne.[37]

In New Zealand also the Catholic establishment was initially hostile to the Rising, and in the New Zealand Tablet it was rubbished as a 'made-in-Germany' rebellion. The socialists of the *Maoriland Worker*, on the other hand, were good friends of Larkin and Connolly, and had campaigned for the Irish Transport and General Workers Union at the time of the Dublin lockout. In its pages Harry Holland lauded the Rising, and gave a talk on 'Ireland's famines and rebellions' to a packed audience at the Alexandra Hall, Wellington, where he was 'applauded and cheered throughout'.

In March of 1917 the *Tablet* changed its editor, and its stance backing Pearse and the Rising. The Dunedin branch of the Irish National Association was militant in its support for the rebels, and a journal it backed, the *Green Ray* was put down by the government, its editor and manager jailed for sedition. A campaign over the banning of the *Green Ray* helped to bring the Irish and Labour closer together. In 1921 the convention of the Irish Self Determination League in Wellington drew a sizeable audience. New Zealanders raised large sums to help the rebel state, and then for relief for the victims of the Belfast riots. When Bishop James Liston of Auckland was prosecuted for sedition for speaking out against British repression, the Supreme Court overturned his sentence on the grounds that it was not sedition in New Zealand.[38]

Irish-America

The strongest popular support for the new Irish Republic, of course, was among Irish-Americans. When de Valera arrived in Boston 1919, 25,000 turned up to greet him at the railway station, and twice that number came out to hear him at a rally on 29 June. A week later 17,000 turned up at an overcrowded Madison Square Gardens, New York, and then later 25,000 saw him in Chicago's Soldier's field, before he went up and down the West Coast. Irish-Americans were well organised, not just in the Church, but as an ethnic lobby that had been alarming Britons since the Fenian challenge of the 1860s. The Irish Republican Brotherhood was well-established and organised as Clan na Gael, led by Joseph McGarrity, who would be an important power-broker for republicans. McGarrity helped organise the Irish Race Conventions, which since the Convention in New York in 1916 had moved from Home Rule to outright support for a Republic. The Irish in America were hostile to the war, which was a limit on de Valera's bargaining power with Woodrow Wilson at the Versailles Treaty. The President of the new Republic was disappointed that Wilson's support for the rights of small nations stopped at the territorial claims of the British Empire.[39]

Chapter four

Revising the Rising

The idea that militant republicanism was fed by ('bad') history is a misunderstanding. The upsurge of support for Sinn Fein in the north in the 1970s was not really down to the appeal of romantic historical tales. Of course it was true that the *United Irishman*, and then later *An Phoblacht/Republican News*, carried stories honouring their heroes, and that anniversaries like 1916 were the occasion of marches and parades. Any movement has its own set of values, and its own account of what is happening, as a counter to the mainstream. Those things were important, to some extent, as ideology – but Conor Cruise O'Brien and Ruth and Owen Dudley Edwards, like Austen Morgan, Paul Bew and Henry Patterson after them, just made too much of this detail of sustaining the movement. It was not what Provisional Sinn Fein had to say about the past that was propelling it forward, but what it had to say about the present.

It was the republicans who held on to the fight for civil rights in the face of repression. The republican movement took up the struggle against internment and challenged the forces that were attacking the nationalist population. For that it won first respect, tacit support, and then outright support. It was uncomfortable for the intelligentsia in Dublin, as it was for those in London, to realise that their own ideas about what should happen had so little impact on the people, and rather than trying to understand how they had misjudged the question, they tried to understand how the people of northern Ireland had let them down. How could you explain the support for republicanism among the Catholics of Derry and Belfast? If it was closed to you to under- stand that they had a case against their oppression, you were forced to argue that they were mesmerised, or in the grip of a mystical and mythical ideology of '800 years of oppression' (a phrase that features in caricatures of republicanism more than it does in their own presses).

So the war of ink went on, a regular Battle of the Books. More and more was written to explain away the appeal of opposition to the British occupation of northern Ireland; more and more volumes bravely scoffing at the supposed heroes of republicanism – heroes who loomed larger in the minds of those who were out to tear them down than anywhere else. The Oedipal assault on the Founding Fathers revealed nothing quite so much as the resentment of the embittered petit bourgeois.

Ruth Dudley Edwards' 1977 biography of Patrick Pearse – subtitled 'the Triumph of Failure' – which had him delivering 'the key to a Pandora's box of troubles', set the mould for the books that followed. Edwards argued that 'Pearse and his friends had left, by their words and their actions, a political legacy which could be construed as a defence of the die-hards'. But the 'Republic proclaimed at Easter 1916 proved to be unattainable', and 'partition could not be avoided'. The problem was that the ideal set by the Rising had dangerous consequences: 'independent Ireland produced intransigent minorities, whose refusal to compromise should hardly have come as a surprise to generations accustomed to the taunt "where were you in 1916?"

Pearse, argues Edwards 'had been consistently disappointed in the response of his countrymen to the visions laid before them', but never wondered whether it was his appeal that was wrong. She says sharply that 'he wrote, acted and died for a people that did not exist'. She said that he had 'mystical yearnings for martyrdom'. Many of these points about Pearse were made at the time, by Connolly and by the IRB leader Bulmer Hobson, whom Edwards quotes saying Pearse was 'a sentimental egotist' who 'became convinced of the necessity for a periodic blood sacrifice to keep the national spirit alive'. Hobson, the organiser, complained that 'he did not contribute greatly to the hard grinding work of building up the movement', but loved the limelight.

Patrick Pearse

Edwards did accept that Pearse's rhetoric of blood was in keeping with much of contemporary political writing, in republican and socialist papers, whose tone had to compete with the growing hysteria of British Army recruitment propaganda. Liam de Paor made a similar point when he said that Pearse's imagery was borrowed from the Imperial traditions of the day. 'Pearse could speak the language of their enemy: this was one of the chief reasons he was chosen, not long before 1916, by those who planned revolution, to be a spokesman and a leader'. The truth was, of course, that Pearse was a fine orator who inspired many, as can be seen, for example, in the funeral speech for O'Donovan Rossa that ends 'Ireland unfree shall never be at peace'. While many took issue with Pearse's talk of spilling blood, he was only quoting Thomas Jefferson, who said 'the tree of liberty must be refreshed from time to time with the blood of patriots and tyrants'. Strangely, few take issue today with the more resolute militarist John Redmond, who recruited tens of thousands to fight in the British Army, to slaughter German conscripts in the trenches and shed their own blood for the Empire – the conflagration that the Rising was seeking to end.[1]

Even the most admirable traits become sinister in Edwards' eyes, as she manages to find fault with Pearse's commitment to education with her clairvoyant discovery that Pearse was a paedophile: 'I pointed out the bleeding obvious – that Pearse, although almost certainly chaste, was turned on exclusively by young male beauty'. As with the posthumous charges that biographers made against Charles Dodgson (who wrote as Lewis Carroll), Edwards had just got confused between the prurient sexualisation of children in her own times and the idealisation of childhood innocence that was common among the middle classes of the Edwardian age.[2]

By the standards of later attacks on the leaders of the Rising, even Ruth Dudley Edwards' *Patrick Pearse* is moderate in its takedown. But in 1977 the standard for biography was still indulgent. The original revenge memoir by Christine Crawford of her mother Joan, *Mommie Dearest*, was not published till the following year. Reviewers in Ireland were shocked or thrilled at the transgressive retelling of this hero of the Rising and his life.

Ruth's brother Owen Dudley Edwards gave a particularly argumentative interpretation of the Rising in his 1987 biography of Éamon de Valera. Making a forced comparison between the leaders of the Easter Rising and the Austrian Archduke's 'Young Bosnia' assassin, Gavrilo Princip, brother Edwards says that 'it unleashed throughout Europe an orgy of self-immolation on the altar of mortal combat'. That was true in a trivial sense, but not really the reason that the war happened, which was already ratcheted up to breaking point before the trigger was pulled in Sarajevo. Still, the coincidence lets Edwards conflate the opponents of the war, the leaders of the Easter Rising, with the warmongers in London and Berlin.

So he claims that 'the Easter insurgents responded to the same mood which led so many to fight for Britain'. Really? The Easter Rising was taken up by supporters of the British Empire? Against all sense, Edwards insists 'the ideals were the same: militarism, honour, patriotism, self-sacrifice, manhood, adventure'. It is an argument wholly formalistic, identifying oppressed and oppressor on the grounds of those formal similarities they shared. That the one was seeking to send Irishmen off to France to fight and die while the other was fighting against the war disappears in Edwards' telling. Instead of seeking to understand the cause of the rebels, he subsumes their action under a preconceived category of 'militarism'. So, he claims, 'Combat and death had become world-wide faiths':

Ireland had taken her place among the nations of the earth. She had simply chosen to do so when the nations of the earth were at the height of suicidal irrationality.[3]

But of course the men of the Rising were not joining up for suicidal irrationality, but seeking to put a stop to it. The national movement they revitalised was one that broke the war, sabotaging the British war effort, stymying conscription, and lighting a beacon for all those rebelling against the slaughter.

Ruth Dudley Edwards went on to write a popular biography of that other leading light of the Easter Rising James Connolly, which was much more favourable to her subject. However, in 1988, another biography, much more critical – even dismissive – was published: Austen Morgan's *James Connolly*. For Morgan, by committing himself to the Rising, Connolly

became a Germanophile, and collaborated with a wartime imperialist state. Connolly had little faith in popular revolutionary activity, and he based his expectations on the

MacNeill Volunteers. The Irish Citizen's Army secured his admission to the Irish Republican Brotherhood's military council, and Connolly went to his death an unapologetic Fenian.[4]

The charge that Connolly was a Germanophile and collaborator is hardly new. Indeed it was made against all opponents of the British war effort, pacifist, socialist or Irish patriot. What part of the slogan Connolly had draped over Liberty Hall, 'We Serve Neither King nor Kaiser' does Morgan not understand?

Austen Morgan's biography of James Connolly is difficult to read because its author rejects the central claim he made, that in Ireland the national and the social revolution go hand in hand. To Morgan this claim is sophistry, and a cover for Connolly's abandonment of socialism in favour of nationalism, or as he puts it, 'historically preposterous, conceptually unstable and ultimately dependent on a mythical Connolly'. Morgan says that 'the thesis of socialist and nationalist "complementarity" is repeatedly advanced by students of Connolly, solely on the basis of his rhetorical statement about social and political freedom being future goals'.[5]

But Morgan does not just make this counter argument. He insists throughout the book that Connolly's position is simply impossible to the extent that he cannot even begin to repeat Connolly's own explanation – as if just writing the words down would be a concession to nationalism. The problem in the work becomes that Morgan is incapable of entering the mind of his subject long enough to give an account of his thinking, so that each step Connolly takes becomes mysterious.

Morgan claims that Connolly passed through many different personas, being variously a socialist, a syndicalist, a labourist and finally a cultural nationalist. For the most part though, these are Morgan's own categories, not really derived from Connolly's thinking, nor understanding the unity of his thought, and at most describing the different conditions that he was working in. So, though Connolly at the turn of the century was building the Irish Socialist Republican Party in Dublin, he was also, and understandably, very active in the campaign against the Boer War, and in disrupting the Victoria's Golden Jubilee, in cooperation with Maud Gonne and other Irish nationalists. But to Morgan, Connolly's extensive campaigning against the British Empire in 1897 does not fit his schema that Connolly was a socialist, not a 'cultural nationalist' at that time, so he talks down these actions, saying that he was only 'trying to reproduce the protest of the Socialist league' – who had campaigned against the centenary in 1887 – and to 'legitimize his socialism' with nationalists, that is compromising his socialist principles. Morgan even goes so far as to criticise 'Connolly's opposition to the monarchy' because he 'failed to challenge the national-separatist conception of a republic'.[6]

Morgan concedes that one of the failings of the socialists in the late 19th century was 'their acceptance of colonial exploitation as the solution to metropolitan social problems and a degeneration of Enlightenment values to Eurocentric racism'. But he is most determined that Connolly should not be accredited 'an advanced critic of imperialism in the late 1890s'. Connolly's opposition to the British Empire's fight to control South Africa, bizarrely, is taken as evidence that he was sympathetic to colonialism (represented by the Boers). Indeed Morgan convicts Connolly, without justice, of 'a Eurocentric and indeed racist view of world politics', saying that 'the people of the "non-civilised" world are *totally missing* in Connolly's writings' – but then contradicting himself to say they appear 'only rhetorically in nationalist reference to the British Empire'. He goes on, falsely, to attribute to Connolly John Dillon's view that the Irish deserved self-government 'because we are white men' – a thought Connolly never once expressed.[7]

The truth is the opposite. Connolly was indeed 'an advanced

critic of imperialism in the 1890s', and more than most socialists, for that reason interested in the condition of subject peoples. For sure, it is his critical attitude to the British Empire that directs him to consider the cases of the Boer 'robbed of his freedom', the Egyptian 'hurled back under the heel of his taskmaster', the Zulu 'dynamited in his caves', the Matabele 'slaughtered beside the ruins of his smoking village or Afridi to be hunted from his desolated homestead' (in the *Workers Republic*, 13 August 1898). Nor could it be said that Connolly's critique of imperialism is restricted to a critique of the British Empire, since he wrote in the *Workers Republic* that it was no better that 'a German capitalist ousts an English capitalist from the chance of swindling some African' (15 October 1889).

Morgan smuggles his own ideas and judgments into the book, unexplained, as if they were incontrovertible facts. So we are told more than once that 'Ireland does not exist', which might be an interesting idea if he would deign to explain it to us, but he does not. That would mean reaching out of the impregnable fortress of correct-thinking that Morgan imagines he inhabits. It would risk compromising his conviction by putting it alongside, even for a moment, the mundane counter view.

Morgan heaps up many harsh – but false – judgments of his subject, Connolly. Connolly he thinks is a bit unlettered, and not really a master of socialist theory (unlike the great thinker Austen Morgan!). Rather, claims Morgan, 'the street was his main arena of intervention where he would preach' socialism, or he was guided by his 'proletarian instincts'. 'He must have wrestled to educate himself during his army service', and 'Connolly possessed a copy of *Capital*, with which he may have struggled', but his mastery of its concepts 'do not stand close examination'.[8] It is a pointedly ignorant judgment of Connolly who, whatever one thinks of his work and its outcome, was very well-read and shows a great command of the socialist and historical materialist canon of his day, and for its times a good command of Irish history, too. What perhaps confuses Morgan is that there are precious few direct citations or sub-clauses or footnotes in Connolly's writings. But that is largely because Connolly wrote socialist agitational propaganda, which had to be blunt, clear and readable (so unlike Austen Morgan's own writing style). Connolly, in contrast to Morgan, wears his learning lightly.

Morgan's reading of his own sources is often misleading. He says that Lenin dismisses the Irish Citizen Army as 'backward workers ... [with] their prejudices and reactionary fantasies, their weaknesses and errors'. But Lenin is not talking about the Irish Citizen Army, nor even strictly about Ireland, but the European socialist revolution, in which, he says, it is bound to be the case that as well as advanced workers, backward workers will take part. Arbitrarily, without foundation, Morgan asserts that this means the Irish Citizen Army.[9] Similarly Morgan appeals to Lenin's authority to characterise the Rising as 'a Putsch', citing the exact article in which Lenin rejects Radek's characterisation of the Rising as a Putsch.

At the core of Morgan's distaste for Connolly is his positive view of 'Ireland's benign colonial rulers'.[10] Pointedly, even the Royal Commission on the Rebellion in Ireland took a more critical view of colonial rule than Morgan's, concluding that 'if the Irish system of Government be regarded as a whole it is anomalous in quiet times and almost unworkable in times of crisis' (3 July 1916). More to the point, there was nothing benign about the Empire's human sacrifice of thousands of Irishmen, Catholics and Protestants alike, and their German and Turkish victims, to the glory of the Nation; nor was there anything benign about the repressive measures that the Lord Lieutenants of Ireland took to silence their republican critics. To Morgan, though, every challenge to British rule can only be understood as an expression of 'nationalism', because he will not look critically at his own Unionist prejudices.

In time for the centenary, the historian Roy Foster wrote a

group biography of the revolutionary generation of 1890–1923. His book *Vivid Faces* draws together a great deal of the psychological analysis of the men and women of 1916. So Pearse is 'histrionic' in whose plays 'homoeroticism is safely diverted into servitude and death'; Terence MacSwiney was 'an autodidactic, obsessive, introspective youth', 'histrionic, frustrated and ambitious'. Many of the Republicans, Foster divines, were of Protestant backgrounds, 'fuelled by a sense of guilt and compensation', or they were sexually frustrated, in some cases, and 'the lesbianism of several key figures was surprisingly unabashed', people for whom 'sexual dissidence ... could be another alienating factor', and for whom 'sexual radicalism, feminism and agit-prop theatre' were motivations. Reading Foster's trolling through the diaries of the generation of 1916, it is surprising to think that they ever got around to making a revolution. His many stories of the unconventional lives of these republicans are supposed to cast them as cranks and weirdoes, though for the most part they just make them seem more interesting and open to new ideas. Where *Vivid Faces* fails as history is in its singular focus on the lives of the literary and artistic intelligentsia, when so many of the men and women of the Rising were not great keepers of diaries or writers of plays and poems. The event's connection to the social upheavals across Europe in the war years is side-lined by Foster's unremittingly psychological focus.[11]

As we have seen, the coterie of anti-republican historians that Morgan was a part of were northerners, rather than southerners like Foster, who were reacting to the arguments over a later conflict than the Easter Rising: the rise of the Civil Rights movement in 1969, and the republican challenge to British rule in the Six Counties of northern Ireland. Austen Morgan, Paul Bew and Henry Patterson all claim to have been supporters of the Civil Rights movement, but reacted against the increasingly nationalist character of the opposition to the Orange State. As their disagreements became sharper, they came to resent the

leaders of the Civil Rights movement and the leading organisation within it, People's Democracy. Austen Morgan calls out
the 'anti-imperialist school of Irish socialism, inspired by the
trinity of McCann, Farrell and Bell' (that's Eamon, Michael and
Geoffrey)[12] – but it is a small church that worships these three as
a trinity, men who have achieved some things in their lives, but
are hardly gods.

At a conference at Warwick University in 1978 Bew, Patterson
and Morgan took on the People's Democracy, including Michael
Farrell. There Paul Bew raised the main theme of the argument
between the pro- and anti-republican left. The core issue was the
attitude to the national question, said Bew, and the 'application
of certain formulations of James Connolly' who 'equated "true"
national revolution with social and economic revolution'. And
from this the conclusion was drawn that 'the revolution of
1918–1921 could be considered incomplete'. Still, thought Bew,
the leaders of People's Democracy 'saw its eventual completion
as a by-product of social revolution, rather than vice versa';
more, they thought that socialism was 'a strictly secular force
which unlike the national question could unite Protestants and
Catholics'.[13]

Unfortunately, says Bew, this view was 'abandoned by its
authors around 1970, as having been obviously mistaken, at least
in its assumption of the reformability of the Northern State'. Bew
quotes an article from the People's Democracy's *Socialist Republic*
paper saying 'we underestimated the importance of the national
question and partition, the violence with which imperialism
would react to the challenge of Civil Rights and therefore the
need for armed defence of the ghettoes' (Vol 1, No 6, 1978).
Eccentrically, Bew reads this accurate assessment as a failure to
understand the state, and 'its fundamental significance as a
unifier of the dominant classes and a divider of the dominated
classes' – perhaps that was true in the first flush of the Civil
Rights movement, but the understanding that the state would

promote sectarianism to defeat the challenge to its power was just what the *Socialist Republic* paper was saying.[14]

Bew took issue with the Civil Rights protestors Farrell and Eamon McCann on the grounds that 'their position departs fundamentally from Lenin's': 'As far as Lenin was concerned there was no abstract right of national self-determination which was to be supported by Socialists on all occasions.' Rather there were 'concrete national questions which were to be evaluated in terms of the interests of the international proletariat'. More, 'the right of specific nations to self-determination was usually supported because it cleared the stage for the development of the class struggle in both "oppressor" and "oppressed" nations'. According to this formula, says Bew, 'the attempt to portray the essence of the struggle in the North as being for National Liberation is misguided'.[15] Austen Morgan complains that one of the reasons that the IRA campaign in the north got a hearing was that 'Britain has many enemies in the world' – well, quite. The record of British imperialism in the world was not so positive that other national liberation movements would fail to recognise the republicans' cause.[16]

No doubt it was a great burden on the Irish Republican Army that they had only read Lenin without the assistance of Professor Bew's annotations. They had failed to understand that the right of small nations for liberation against imperialism – a struggle that Lenin himself had so pointedly associated with social revolution – did not truly apply in their conflict. But then it was not really the case that the struggle in the north of Ireland was principally inspired by Lenin, or even Connolly, but by the military clampdown, beginning with the attacks on the Civil Rights march, the internment of republicans and socialists in 1971, and the subsequent armed attacks on the nationalist population. That Irish people should wish to be rid of British rule really does not need so grand, or tortuous, an explanation.

One of the key points of difference that Bew raises against

Michael Farrell and Eamon McCann is that they abandoned the strategy of winning over Protestant workers. Bew says that: 'the whole of the decade prior to 1968 had been characterised by secular class conflicts within the Protestant bloc which arose originally as a result of the severe recession in Belfast between 1958 and 1962'. What's more, 'important sections of the Protestant working class moved towards the Northern Ireland Labour Party'. Also 'through the medium of the Northern Ireland Labour Party sections of the working class frequently opposed the Unionist bourgeoisie in secular class terms' – a good thing, according to the Paul Bew of 1978.

Bew in particular takes issue with an argument he finds in Michael Farrell's book *The Orange State*, that the institutions of loyalism and the government of the Six Counties have limited militancy amongst Protestant workers. Farrell had argued that the Ulster Unionists had 'secured the allegiance of the Protestant workers by a systematic policy of discrimination against Catholics', and 'as the "aristocrats of labour" with secure jobs in heavily subsidised industries dependent on British markets, they are the staunchest opponents of a united Ireland'. Bew notes that 'difficulties surround this notion of an "aristocracy of labour"' (and it is true that Farrell only really uses the phrase metaphorically, not directly aligning it with the concept in labour history). Bew insists that 'this social class was no more obviously bought off by the differentials which existed than the Catholic working class was revolutionised by them'. Bew adds, rather interestingly, that 'it is bourgeois sociology, not Marxism, which attaches primacy to differences in the sphere of distribution and the labour market rather than those in the realm of production'.[17]

The quest to find a progressive dimension to the self-organisation of the Protestant working class has been a powerful motivation for this trio of writers, which has produced a lot of books, such as Patterson's *Class conflict and sectarianism: The protestant working class and the Belfast labour movement 1868–1920*;

Morgan's *Labour and Partition: The Belfast Working Class 1905–1923* (London, 1991); and more recently Patterson's *Unionism and Orangeism in Northern Ireland Since 1945* (with Eric Kaufmann, Manchester, 2007) – and see also Ruth Dudley Edwards' *The Faithful Tribe* (London, 1999).

There is no doubt that these researches have greatly increased our understanding of the contours and predicaments of the loyalists of northern Ireland, and there is a great deal to be applauded here. One thing that is difficult to gainsay, though, is that all of these studies have tended to give more and more evidence to support the view that the institutions of loyalism, the Orange Order, the Ulster Unionist Council, the Ulster Unionist Party and their intimate relation to the governing institutions have indeed tended to bind northern Ireland's Protestants closely to the State, and also to put definite limits on their room for independent action.

Henry Patterson and Eric Kaufmann's use of the Ulster Unionist Council's records in particular gives a strong insight into the struggles within loyalism. The wartime complaints from Orange lodges against 'a proposal that recruitment of labour be transferred from the control of Councillors to the Labour Exchange', the authors explain, stemmed from the fear that this would make 'it more difficult for party supporters to get employment'. Further, complaints were laid against the recruitment of Catholics to war industries as 'it would be difficult if not impossible to remove these people at the end of the war as they would have dug themselves well in'.

So far from being a source of progressive social change, this poisonous alliance was an actual barrier to economic development. In 1956 Unionist MP Edward Jones warned that 'industrial expansion is a most dangerous thing', and that all projects should be considered from the point of view of 'how the labour force which such projects will involve can be supplied so as to maintain and safeguard the Loyalist majority'.[18] It seemed then that – bourgeois sociology apart – the loyalist stranglehold on labour recruitment was indeed a question of production as well as one of distribution. Patterson, Morgan and Bew all outline many instances of militancy among loyalist workers' organisations, but in all of these the conflict between the employers and the workers are either contained or redirected into attacks on Catholics.

At the Warwick University talk in 1978 Paul Bew appealed that socialists in northern Ireland should aim 'for the construction of a progressive alliance to reform the state and create the best possible conditions for the class struggle' and that 'primacy should be given to reducing the extent of the divisions among the masses themselves'.[19] But this was to ignore the actual struggle that was unfolding between the nationalist population and the state, and give primacy to a movement that existed largely in the minds of Paul Bew and a handful of optimistic 'progressive' Unionists.

For Morgan and the rest the real blame for the reactionary turn in Unionism came from republicanism. It was, they argue, the pressing of the republican claim that fed the Unionists' reaction. In a sense that is true, in the way that all revolutionary movements provoke reaction, in the same way that the rise of the left in Europe provoked the rise of fascist gangs, or the upsurge of industrial militancy in southern Europe and Latin America in the 1970s provoked a series of military coups. The real responsibility for the reaction, though, lay with the loyalist leaders and their apologists.

When Sinn Fein split in the 1970s the breakaway militant faction (the Provisionals) were determined to take the fight to the British Army in occupation of northern Ireland. The 'Officials' were dismayed that their long-term strategy of winning support amongst organised labour was jeopardised by this turn to conflict. Increasingly, the Officials lost perspective in their debate with their former comrades, murdering many of them, and then collaborating with the security services in their elimination – 'it was only the state forces which could defeat Provisionalism' said the Officials' leader Sean Garland. The group was renamed 'Sinn Fein the Workers Party', and then just the 'Workers Party'. The Officials' Eamon Smullen recruited Bew and Patterson to help write the organisation's new doctrine, as the leaders were trying to turn it from a radical nationalist to a 'socialist' organisation. That meant that they were schooled in an ideological struggle against nationalism, in a rather hot-house atmosphere: a faction, within an organisation that still had a military wing, seeking to find a foothold in the trade union movement (and also the media) while still grappling with the attentions of the state security forces, and the embittered reaction of veteran republicans. These were all experiences that developed some pretty insular group-think, with a propensity for speaking in the abbreviated code and adhering to dogmatic claims that is characteristic of people who have been working up ideas in isolation.[20]

Looking back today it is strange to think of this particular coterie dismissing republicanism from the point of view of socialism. In truth their 'socialism' was pretty cranky, even in the 1980s. Bew and Patterson both took part in the 1984 Marx Centenary organised by the Workers Party; Patterson was writing articles for the Workers Party and later for another breakaway, Democratic Left, that lauded Joseph Stalin as a serious thinker, and made the positive case for 'class reductionism'. The socialism of this group, though, turned out to be much more ephemeral than the ghosts of 1916. They barked from their socialist redoubts about who had read Lenin or Marx right, but mostly about how idealistic the republicans were. This 'socialism' had no real content other than as a platform from which to attack republi-canism. Once it had served its purpose it melted away, demanding no great sacrifice or labour from its adherents, and certainly not standing in the way of their later alliances with the powers-that-be.

Today Paul Bew is in the House of Lords, Baron Bew of Donegore, and has been advisor to the (former) Ulster Unionist Party leader David Trimble. Henry Patterson was a signatory of the Euston Manifesto in 2003 in support of Western intervention in the Middle East. Austen Morgan has since qualified as a barrister, doing mostly commercial work, but he does have an interest in 'human rights'. His contribution to the collection of essays *Combating Terrorism in Northern Ireland* dismisses the many criticisms of the suspension of legal process in northern Ireland during the troubles. In the face of such examples as the killings undertaken by the state security force, internment without trial, trials without juries, security service collusion with loyalist paramilitaries in assassinations of political critics, and the ubiquitous use of spies, paid informants, blackmail and surveillance, Morgan concludes that 'the UK, by and large, observed the rule of law during the troubles' (echoing his earlier judgment of 'Ireland's benign colonial rulers'). 'Emergency legislation', like the infamous Prevention of Terrorism Act, 'is not contrary to human rights'. To Morgan's irritation, not all human rights lawyers, and in particular those in the Committee on the Administration of Justice founded in Belfast in 1981, agree with his sunny view of British rule in northern Ireland. His judgment is 'The NI human rights community: an infantile disorder' (a reference to Lenin's pamphlet *Left Wing Communism: An Infantile Disorder*, an in-joke to no-one in particular to say that he still sees himself as Lenin, hunting down the deviationists). Their crime? That they criticise the British authorities when they should be criticising republicans. While Morgan was denouncing human rights lawyers in northern Ireland, the security forces, in collusion with Protestant paramilitaries, had two of them, Pat Finucane and Rosemary Nelson, assassinated.[21]

Historical revisionism is not a very useful term. For a start, it suggests that the new revised version will be superior to the unrevised, but that is not always the case. The image it sums up is of a mainstream of nationalist historical writing that is only now being challenged by young and brave historians. But just when was the turn against this supposed mainstream of nationalist writing? Was it in the 1980s with Bew, Patterson and Morgan, or was it in the 1970s with Ruth and Owen Dudley Edwards and Conor Cruise O'Brien? In 1972 Owen Dudley Edwards made claims for 'a school of writers from both sides of the Irish border who resolutely sought objectivity, detachment and the salvation of professional academic history from the political battleground'. Roy Foster talked about the 'soi disant "revisionist" school of Irish historians, who since the 1940s have been dispassionately re-evaluating the assumptions of the eight-hundred years of struggle version of Irish history'. T.W. Moody and Robert Dudley Edwards are generally credited with this innovation, and in *Irish Historical Studies*, the journal Moody edited, the sub-heading 'Historical Revision' was commonly used on articles that proposed a new interpretation of an historical event.[22]

Even further back, of course, the pro-Treaty intellectuals associated with Fine Gael numbered many important historians, such as James Hogan, Michael Tierney and Eoin MacNeill. As well as being the Irish Volunteer leader who countermanded the Easter Rising, a decision he defended, and which was defended for him by his son-in-law Tierney, MacNeill was a relatively important historian of Ireland at the time of the Anglo-Norman rule; against the received opinion MacNeill showed that Ireland at that time was by no means a unitary state, and the High Kingship was 'not at all the great central institution so often invoked by popular historians'. This was in a series of lectures published in 1919 as *Phases of National History*.[23]

The revision of Irish history has as one might expect been going on as long as history has been studied in Ireland. Historians like to summon up a caricature of the dim-witted older generation, with their stodgy, traditional and ideological 'national history', the better to motivate their own, supposedly iconoclastic, innovative and critical 'post-national' researches. Locating 'national history' in the past and post-national history as innovative, though, is not really true. By casting the anti-national history as 'revisionist' those writers who do not dismiss the claims of nationhood are cast as dogmatists and reactionaries, stuck in the past. Some, like Desmond Fennell and Seamus Deane have accepted the terms of the debate as set out and tried to take on what they call 'revisionism'. Their points are often useful, but overall they pay too high a price when they agree to be seated in the 'anti-revisionist' camp. History is revised all the time, and to be an 'anti-revisionist' is as empty of meaning as to be a 'revisionist'. The terms of the debate themselves are wrong. Nor is it the case that the critique of nationalism is daringly in the margins. Arguably the universities have produced a lot more anti-national history than laudatory hymns to the founding fathers. Anti-national history is the mainstream.

There are, however, writers of history who are sympathetic to republicanism and broadly sympathetic to the Easter Rising. These are not by and large university lecturers, but popular writers, often from the margins, like C. Desmond Greaves (author of fine biographies of Connolly and Liam Mellows), or Tom Jackson, author of *Ireland Her Own*, both leftists, or the novelist Peter Berresford Ellis, who wrote *A History of the Irish Working Class*, or, of course, they are participants in the republican movement who have written memoirs, like Tom Barry, Florence Donohue, Ernie O'Malley, or more latterly, Brendan Behan, Eamon McCann, Michael Farrell and Tommy McKearney. Robert Dudley Edwards' son Owen wrote patronisingly of 'Mr Timothy Patrick Coogan', an 'editor of the *Irish Press*', and his 'volume, *Ireland since the Rising*, whose comparative lack of subtlety makes it a very helpful source of raw material on recent Ireland'. Tim Pat Coogan, of course, is a popular historian, who writes strong narrative history that is broadly sympathetic to the republican cause – which calls forth the snob in the academic historian Dudley Edwards. Similarly Roy Foster complains of how little the 'revisionist' school has affected 'the popular version of Irish history held by the public mind'.[24]

Republican mural, Beechmount Avenue: the kind of unofficial history the academics dread

At its heart, the real contest in Irish history-writing is not between daring revisionists and an established nationalist mainstream. Rather academic historians, in keeping with the outlook of the Irish intelligentsia throughout much of the 20th century, recoil somewhat from nationalism because it is popular. Their distaste for the Easter Rising and the national movement it gave rise to comes from a fear of the masses in history, which is why though they want to preserve an Irish cultural identity, they also identify with the British authorities' struggle to subdue the risen people.

Where the revisionists had a point... and where they did not

The strongest card in the 'revisionist' hand is their showing that Ireland's first head of state Éamon de Valera used the Rising to sanctify the 26-country republic. 'De Valera himself officiated in his priestly function with austerity and dignity', writes Owen Dudley Edwards, to create a 'martyrology'. The criticisms levelled by Edwards and also by Paul Bew and Henry Patterson have a point. The Dublin government hid its failings behind a cult of phoney nationalism. Their further point is that de Valera followed an autarkic economic policy, shutting his country off from modernity, paying a high cost in cultural backwardness, the privileged position of the Church, and the lack of women's rights. Bew and Patterson contrast de Valera unfavourably with his successor Sean Lemass, who 'saw foreign capital and technique as essential to Ireland's continued industrialisation'.[25]

De Valera's social policy was backward, and relied on the Catholic Church to do the job of giving welfare to the destitute, and running the schools. Indeed, the Irish people overall were nowhere near as revolutionary as the record of 1916 to 1921 would suggest. Rather the great mass of people would more often have taken the more cautious choice if it was offered. They would have supported Redmond, but for conscription. When people flocked to Sinn Fein they pulled it to the centre, and to the Treaty. They voted for de Valera in 1932 because he had the authority to stop the drift to violence – both from the Irish Republican Army and the 'blueshirt' rightist militia raised against them. In any event de Valera's return brought only a symbolic campaign against partition but a real accommodation to the south's now shrunken industrial base and its rural bias. De Valera's economic policy was for self-sufficiency ('ourselves alone'), but it was hardly remarkable for that, in the years from 1932 to 1959, when most of the world had erected great trade barriers against each other. Self-sufficiency was a policy helped by Britain's 'economic war'.

De Valera did tend to turn the rebellious spirit of the Rising into a dead sainthood; his 1966 parade looks like the pageantry of Stalinism seen from today, because it did have something of that appeal to obedience in the citizenry on the ground of the sacrifice of the men of the Rising. But that is not true to the Rising; it is itself an act of historical revisionism. These later 'historical revisionists' take de Valera's caricaturing of 1916 to be the real thing, and then rail against that. Bew and Patterson argue that de Valera's economic and social policy was the fulfilment of the goals of the proclamation, but in truth it was their distortion. De Valera's oppressive state had the same relation to the Rising as Stalin's did to the Russian revolution, or Napoleon's to the French: it was the Thermidor, the reaction, wearing the clothes of the revolution. This is what the historian Roy Foster describes as 'the sharply conservative aftermath of the revolution, when nascent ideas of certain kinds of liberation were aggressively subordinated to the national project of restabilization (and clericalization)'.[26]

The social policy of the Rising was far-reaching in its priority for equal opportunities, for social ownership and liberty, showing the input from James Connolly and Constance Markiewicz. Over time, though, the Irish people were exhausted by change, and cowed by military rule and then civil war. First Cosgrave offered stability through compromise, and then de Valera offered the ghost of a Republic on an insular Free State.

Connolly had predicted that partition would lead to 'a carnival of reaction on both sides of the border', and it did. Ireland's social backwardness was felt by all. The Republican argument that the failings of the Free State derive from partition, though, is just what Bew and Patterson are trying to dismiss when they point to Lemass' openness to foreign investment. They are saying that the national revolution is complete; that the modern, 26-county Ireland is a country to itself, and there is no need to challenge partition. It is an argument that first pulls one way, saying that Ireland is backward, proving the pointlessness of nationalism, and then on the other hand claims that Ireland has modernised and is free; it gives an alternative account of why Ireland was underdeveloped – de Valera's ideological commitment to self-sufficiency; and then modernised by Lemass's turn to overseas markets and investors. In the 1990s it looked as if Ireland's 'Celtic tiger' economy had overcome the injuries of partition; though today there is less confidence about the terms on which Ireland's economy has been integrated into the world market.

Too much history

Throughout the years of conflict between Britain and Ireland, the so-called 'historical revisionist' school has chimed happily with the belief among those making the British case that the Irish are unduly preoccupied with history. That the Irish have 'too much history' is a cliché today. It was a complaint British negotiators made against Éamon de Valera that he would take them painstakingly through every year of Anglo-Irish relations going back to the Anglo-Norman conquest of 1169. Moaning about the return of de Valera to government, the Secretary of State for India, Leopold Amery, said that the trouble in Ireland was due to the 'predominance of a party unwilling to forget the past'. Margaret Thatcher repeated the complaint after negotiating the 1985 Anglo-Irish agreement with Charles Haughey, saying that 'I felt at the end I had gained insight into every one of those eight-hundred years'.[27]

Times columnist A. P. Ryan claimed that 'when the guns go

off' the Irish hear:

> echoes of the Black and Tan shootings, the firing in the streets
> of Dublin at Easter, 1916, and other dramatic occasions –
> forgotten or never known about by the British – going back to
> the bloody business of 1798 and to Cromwell. Yes, to
> Cromwell. Incredible though it seems to Britons with their
> mercifully short memories, history stays green in Ireland,
> even after the lapse of centuries.[28]

It was a theme taken up by Denis Ryan, talking about the
shootings on 'Bloody Sunday', 30 January 1972, and the enquiry
that followed. He complained that 'the Irish seem to absorb dates
and historical events with their mothers' milk'. Though he went
on to claim that 'the schools, the Catholic church, the political
parties in the Dáil, the extra parliamentary groups like Sinn Fein
and rural and urban folklore instil historical fact and fantasy to
each generation'. This was how Sinn Fein 'claim to be the true
heirs to the Easter Rising'. It is because of an 'over simplified
verdict that the British role in Ireland has always been aggressive,
punitive and divisive [that] Irish Nationalists reject Lord
Widgery's assessment of the Londonderry shootings': 'folk
history predisposes people to expect that the British indulge in
the occasional massacres of the native Irish' – though few today
would argue with the conclusion that thirteen men were shot
dead in a massacre on Bloody Sunday. On the 80th anniversary of
the Rising, Fintan O'Toole wrote an article, 'Easter Charade' in
the *Observer* that 'the Rising created a heroic mythology that
drives Irish politics to this day', and that 'the religious imagery
and the vivid theatricality helped to lift the Easter rising out of
history and into myth'.[29]

American or German diplomats would smile at hearing that
the English are forgetful of history. Americans are constantly
reminded that Britain has thousands of years of history, whereas

the USA has a mere two hundred or so, while German diplomats complain that the British are still fighting the Second World War. Just as many years passed in Britain since 1169 as did in Ireland, and our head of state holds a title that dates back to 400 A.D., honoured in ceremony on a regular basis.

The idea that the Irish nationalists are wedded to ancient historical grudges is a misunderstanding of the way that history is read and historical events observed. Historical observance plainly is important to all kinds of movements, including republicans and loyalists, British Army regiments, socialist parties and trades unions, governments and right-wing parties. In observing moments in history, like the Easter Rising, the Great War or the transportation of the Tolpuddle Martyrs, communities of interest are doing more than disinterested reading; they are emphasising their connection to each other by emphasising their connection to the past. The mistake, though, is to imagine that the historical accounts are themselves a motivating power. They are rather the means through which people understand their present-day loyalties, strengths and predicaments. When the nationalists of the northern Six Counties marched to the Roger Casement Park to remember the 50th anniversary of the Easter Rising, they were honouring a version of history that marked them out from the official commemorations of the Great War. A reading of history helped them to understand their present predicament, as a less free section of the community, and gave them heart, as they could see themselves as part of a larger story, where courage triumphs over adversity.

From the somewhat cold and distant outlook of Dublin 4 or the Westminster village the force of that historical memory is misunderstood. To those whose are without sympathy for the feeling of solidarity among the marchers, the real relationship is stood on its head. To Conor Cruise O'Brien, or Margaret Thatcher, it seems as if that community is in the grip of historical myth, driven by ancient ghosts. The truth is the opposite. The community is driven by its present-day experiences, which it seeks to understand, or just to feel, through historical commemoration. The wish that all this history would just go away is based on a confusion. The crowds were not really driven by the ghosts of Pearse and Connolly, but by the discrimination in work, housing, policing and government.

Chapter five

Historical memory and the peace process

2016 also sees the 20th anniversary of the end of an IRA ceasefire, marked by the bombings of the Docklands financial district in East London, and Manchester's town centre. These last major acts of the republican bombing campaign in England were followed by another ceasefire the following year. Talks between the political parties in northern Ireland, including Sinn Fein, and the leaders of the British and Irish governments under the auspices of US representative George Mitchell ended with the Good Friday Agreement, on 10 April 1998. The guiding principle of the agreement was that the two traditions – nationalist and unionist – in the Six Counties would have 'parity of esteem' in the eyes of the authorities.

Under the Good Friday Agreement loyalist and nationalist parties agreed to share power in a new Northern Ireland Assembly, in tandem with measures to release paramilitary prisoners, decommission arms and other 'confidence building' measures. The Northern Ireland Assembly was innovative in its power-sharing mechanisms which aimed to stop the representatives of one community from capturing political offices.

One unintended consequence of these power-sharing measures is that the state in northern Ireland has institutionalised the 'nationalist' and 'unionist' political identities, since all members of the legislative assembly must adopt 'a designation of identity, being "Nationalist", "Unionist" or "Other"'. These designations are used to impose a share of posts under the complex mathematics of the 'd'Hondt system'. Also certain acts of the assembly must secure cross-community support, meaning a majority among both unionist and nationalist representatives.

It is worth remembering that the republicanism of Connolly,

Pearse and the other volunteers who fought in the Easter Rising did not recognise or accept the concept of 'two traditions'. They were universalist in their conception of a unified people, be they Catholic, Protestant or Dissenter. They followed in that tradition laid down by Wolfe Tone. It is unfortunate that today, 100 years down the line, Irish republicanism has shifted from this universalist, socialist and enlightenment position to accept the notion of identity politics and 'two traditions'. Though possibly well intentioned, the language of two traditions, two cultures and two identities has not advanced politics, but rather has reinforced division. The sad irony is that it is the very discourse of the peace process via the politics of cultural difference and parity of esteem that has essentialised separation between Catholics and Protestants in the Six Counties, rather than unified them.

Though the end of the military conflict in northern Ireland was almost universally welcomed, the practical effects of the Good Friday Agreement have not overcome the sectarian divide between Catholic and Protestant communities, but rather entrenched them. Asking the political representatives to identify as nationalist or unionist, and then sharing out ministerial posts on that basis, means that all competition, whether for resources or standing, becomes a competition between communities.

An interesting analysis of Social Policy adopted by the Northern Ireland Assembly finds they agreed on 'relatively small amount of new legislation in areas of devolved powers', but that for the most part strategies were already outlined for them in either statutory duties under UK government legislation, in European Union directives or in international agreements. Ann Marie Gray and Derek Birrell point to 'the "disconnect" between politics, democracy and the public in Northern Ireland'.[1]

Issues of material competition are largely contained by Westminster-derived legislation, like the Fair Employment and Treatment (Northern Ireland) Order 1998, which, following the 1989 Fair Employment legislation, has greatly curtailed the old system of sectarian job allocation. On top of that of all UK regions, northern Ireland has the highest public-sector employment as a percentage of total employment (27.9% – and the highest public expenditure per head) and moderating unemployment (at 6.3%, still much higher than in the UK average of 3.2%). Though moderated in employment, sectarian divisions have if anything become more entrenched in the separation of the communities by area, with Belfast divided by 26 miles of 'peace walls'.

What the terms of the Good Friday Agreement cannot do is to satisfy nationalist ambitions for a reunited Ireland. The armed struggle of the IRA did not achieve the removal of British rule in the Six Counties, or remove partition. However, it did effectively gain equality and equal rights for the nationalist population. Nonetheless, the result of continued partition means that when nationalists and republicans commemorate the Easter Rising, there is a particular sadness and poignancy, linked to the fact that the Six Counties was left behind when the Irish Free State achieved a measure of independence. This is a fact few Dublin politicians ever bother to remark upon when alluding to the anniversary of the Easter Rising.

All the same the 'confidence building' measures have gone a long way to mitigate the identification of the state with the loyalist community – most pointedly in the renaming of the Royal Ulster Constabulary as the Police Service of Northern Ireland. The question must be asked however – is it really a great victory to have more Catholics in a police force, whose main aim at the end of the day is to maintain partition and administer British rule? It's probably unwise to invoke the dead, but one wonders if this arrangement stops some way short of what the freedom fighters of 1916 would have settled for. Most of these confidence-building measures deal with symbolic goods rather than material ones, like the badges on the policemen's caps. Moreover, many policies aimed at peace and reconciliation revolve around questions of history and commemoration, creating the unanticipated outcome that historical memory is perhaps even more politicised, and contested, than it was during the open violence of 'the Troubles'.

Overall the British government has tried to use the peace process to re-establish their authority over the province. By seeming to stand above the conflict, even attacking their former loyalist allies, they are seeking to re-establish their status as honest brokers between two warring factions. Conceding past faults shores up the power of the state today.

The Independent Commission on Policing for Northern Ireland, known as the Patten Commission, began a broad process of consultation, inviting communities to share their thoughts and experiences of the Royal Ulster Constabulary. Nationalist communities vented their frustration at their past treatment at the hands of the RUC, and Patten soaked up the anger. Journalist Beatrix Campbell noted that 'Protestants addressed the meetings in mournful lament for the old order, disengaged from any

Loyalists against the state – Drumcree, 1997.
Picture credit: Mark McCormick

debate about the future police service'.[2]

This would become a pattern: that the loyalist community were the refuseniks of the peace process, complaining that the nationalists played their hand rather better. James Connolly made the point that whereas in the rest of the world Protestants had been the radicals and Catholics the conservatives, in Ireland it was the other way around (*Forward*, 3 May, 1913). Now, under the peace process, nationalists' leaders, at least, have become the more enthusiastic defenders of the new dispensation, the loyalists the grumpy rebels.

The Patten Commission ended with an agreement to hire as many Catholics as Protestants, to appoint an independent Police Ombudsman, and, of course, to rename the force the Police Service of Northern Ireland.

In 1998 Prime Minister Tony Blair set up the Saville Enquiry into the events on Bloody Sunday when the paratroopers regiment shot dead thirteen protestors. The Enquiry began to take evidence in 2000 and its final report was given to the Northern Ireland Secretary Owen Patterson in 2010. For all the thoroughness of the investigation, not much new was added to our understanding. The main difference was that the official judgment of the previous Widgery Enquiry, which whitewashed the massacre, was overturned. Cynics pointed out that the £400 million cost of the Enquiry had made a few lawyers millionaires while the Ministry of Defence has offered each of the families of the victims just £50,000 in compensation.

The importance of the enquiry, however, was that it released the pressure of historical events in a way that was controlled by the British authorities. Those who complained that the task was dragging were missing the point. The longer the enquiry took, the less drama attached to its findings. Lord Saville successfully released the tension from this historical event. What had been a focus for protests against the state now became the basis of a reassertion of state power. Here was a case of managing the historical record, with the goal of achieving the reconciliation of aggrieved families with the powers-that-be. Owen Patterson said in the House of Commons that 'Helping families and wider society achieve greater understanding and closure is vital, however difficult that may be.'

In 1954 Parliament passed the Flags and Emblems Act which empowered the Royal Ulster Constabulary to take down any national flag – apart from the Union Jack – likely to cause a breach of the peace. In practise this meant that Irish tricolours were regularly taken down (though not from 12th of July bonfires) while the Union Flag was all over. It was a petty but deeply-felt display of loyalist supremacy, exercised most pointedly in workplaces and government offices. In 2013 the Department for Culture, Media and Sport put out guidelines setting out which eighteen days of the year government buildings ought to show the flag. At Stormont officials interpreted that to mean that it should not fly over the castle for the rest of the year, and loyalists rioted at the implied surrender. It was another sign that the heraldry and symbolism of the Orange State would no longer be supported from Westminster. Once again the struggle over symbolic goods generated greater conflict than that over material ones.

Another important body for managing the public commemoration of historical events was the Parades Commission set up under the Public Processions (Northern Ireland) Act 1998. Northern Ireland's marching season was often a test of strength, as Nationalists honoured the Easter Rising and the Bloody Sunday massacres, while the Orange Order geared up to commemorate the Twelfth (of July, 1690, anniversary of William's victory over King James at the Boyne). Parades were seen as a focus for sectarian conflict, but loyalists were shocked to find that their baiting of nationalists, televised, found them few friends in England. The Parades Commission began to lay down rules about routes of marches, and communities set out their complaints against marches that brought unruly mobs to their doors. Unused to negotiating loyalists' more often lost out, and more often protested the decisions of the Parades Commission. When they were warned that they were coming across as block-headed bigots, loyalists told Ruth Dudley Edwards 'we are blockheaded bigots'. Once again the basic dynamic was that the majority community was losing its privileges, and the state enhancing its authority by enforcing 'parity of esteem'. But just as importantly, the government control of historical memory was being reasserted. As commemoration served the goals of Protestant supremacy in the past, today it would serve the goals of reconciliation.

In 2006 Secretary of State Peter Hain established the Consultative Group on the Past – inspired by the South African 'Truth and Reconciliation Commission'. But the Consultative Group was not committed to the truth – rather to managing historical facts to suit an agenda of conformity. In 2009 they reported that

The past should be dealt with in a manner which enables society to become more defined by its desire for true and lasting reconciliation, rather than by division and mistrust, seeking to promote a shared and reconciled future for all.

The Group took issue with those 'many during the consultation process [who] believed that we cannot change the past'. We *can* change the past, they were arguing; if not its facts, at least the meaning put upon those facts.

The way that the Consultative Group saw the issue repeated the stereotypes of Irish people in the grip of ancient prejudices. They thought that 'Buried memories fester in the unconscious minds of communities in conflict, only to emerge later in even more distorted and virulent forms to poison minds and relationships'. Once again, real conflict in the present was being dressed up as a hangover from the past. The Consultative Group's way is very different, though, from those who wanted to stop the commemoration of the past. The new approach is to get it all out in the open, and vent the memories – as they say, 'forgetfulness plays no useful part in true forgiveness'.[3]

Early in 2014 Kathryn Stone gave a talk on her recent appointment as the Commissioner for Victims and Survivors in Northern Ireland – a position created by Secretary of State Peter Hain in 2005. She said that 'there must never be a hierarchy of pain' – which takes some unpacking. She was responding to the 'many in Northern Ireland who believe there should be a hierarchy of victims, that there are innocent victims and that "victim makers" should not be included in the definition of the victim'. Stone suggests that 'maybe what is really being talked about, it has been suggested, is a hierarchy of blame'. But

> the tears of the victim's mother are the same colour as those of the mother of the man who set the bomb. No one wins; everyone hurts.

Hence, there must never be a hierarchy of pain. The tone of the comments is democratic and broad, in that all must be included in the collective victimisation, even those who set the bomb. She goes on to describe an exchange with a former Royal Ulster Constabulary officer:

> At the end of his clearly upsetting description of what he had seen, what he had heard and what he had experienced, he said, "We are all victims here, love".[4]

Considered through the prism of victimisation and suffering the distinctions between the freedom fighter/terrorist and the law officer/oppressor all disappear. Equality is attained amongst victims. But the cost of the manoeuvre is high. The solidarity of victimisation gets rid of responsibility, and by implication conscious choice over your actions. It is the solidarity of the dead.

The very same way of thinking is behind the argument that it is wrong to make a moral distinction between the freedom fighters of the Easter Rising who fought against British imperialism, and those misguided Irishmen who fought on the side of British imperialism. To insist on a moral equivalence is to rob individual agents of free will and the ability to make conscious decisions. This pivotal point strikes at the heart of the problem when it comes to a reluctance on the part of some to make clear moral distinctions about right and wrong. Deploying the rhetoric of victimhood and suffering simply confuses history and leads us down the cul-de-sac of non-judgementalism and relativism. To be clear, the men and women of the Easter Rising were not victims, sectarians or terrorists – they were heroes, freedom fighters and universalists.

The Decade of Centenaries as an extension of the peace process

Faced with the challenge of how to commemorate the Easter Rising the Irish Government is clearly aware that the anniversary has proved so difficult in the past. Whether it is seen as having raised republican ambitions in 1966, or having lost control to Sinn Fein in Dublin in 1976, or just becoming a headache in 1991, the centenary of the Rising presents problems for the administration.

The way that the Easter Rising Commemoration is being planned for in 2016 owes a great deal to the peace and reconciliation model trailed in the Six Counties. The government in Dublin did, after all, take part in the Good Friday Agreement, and joined North-South Joint bodies for ministers and politicians. The Dublin government has been watching the way that the British government enhanced its authority by triangulating between the nationalist and unionist traditions, and lowering the aspirations of its own supporters.

To manage the 2016 commemoration the government in Dublin has set up a Decade of Centenaries programme run by the Department of the Arts, Heritage and the Gaeltacht. The basic idea of the Decade of the Centenaries is to bundle all the centenaries – the Easter Rising, and also the Battle of the Somme, the Dublin lockout and even the signing of the Ulster Covenant – in an ecumenical melange that accommodates every event and tradition, and privileges none.

The Decade of Centenaries all-party committee is chaired by Arts Minister Heather Humphries, whose Presbyterian roots made her a canny, symbolic choice for the role of reconciling the traditions of nationalism, republicanism and unionism. As well as an 'All-Party' committee, the 'Decade of Centenaries' has an advisory committee of historians.

Lord Bew and Minister Deenihan celebrate John Redmond's Home Rule Bill in the House of Commons

The initial statement by the Decade of Centenaries advisory panel of historians says:

The commemoration will be measured and reflective, and will be informed by a full acknowledgement of the complexity of historical events and their legacy, of the multiple readings of history, and of the multiple identities and traditions which are part of the Irish historical experience.

They go on to say that 'there must be full acknowledgement of the multiple identities and traditions which are part of the overall story and of the different ideals and sacrifices associated with them'. Making little secret of the propagandistic meaning of the events, they say that 'the aim should be to broaden sympathies, without having to abandon loyalties, and in particular recognising the value of ideals and sacrifices, including their cost'.

In effect the founding event of the Irish state is to be demoted, lost in a whole forest of centenaries.

They do make the point that 'the State should not be expected to be neutral about its own existence'; but that begs the question how they ever got to the point that this should have to be said?

There is, still, a waspish denunciation of the men of 1916 from the historian advisors who cannot resist saying that the Easter Rising 'represented a direct challenge to constitutionalism and the rule of law'. But overall it is to be celebrated alongside all the other events. That way the government washes its hand of the whole affair, letting anyone who wants to take part in events celebrating Easter 1916, or the Battle of the Somme, or the Dublin lockout – and even the 1912 Covenant to oppose Home Rule by force of arms. It is a very ecumenical approach. But it is not the approach of a government of a sovereign state. Even Germany takes more pride in its national past than Ireland.

The basic outline of the Decade of Centenaries approach was first tried at the 90th anniversary of the Easter Rising in 2006. The statement from John Bruton's government back then was simpler, saying that it 'is committed to respecting all traditions on this island equally'. In 2006 the Taoiseach had already decided that historical events are an opportunity for teaching lessons about getting along: 'developing a greater understanding of our shared history, in all of its diversity, is essential to developing greater understanding and building a shared future'. The government in 2006 also sought to downgrade the Easter Rising, but more bluntly set 'the 90th anniversary of the 1916 Rising in Dublin at Easter and the anniversary of the Battle of the Somme with a ceremony at the war memorial in Islandbridge on July 1st'.[5]

In 2012 the Irish Taoiseach Enda Kenny made a joint

statement with British Prime Minister David Cameron. There the two leaders agreed that 2012 'marks the beginning of a decade of centenary commemorations of events that helped shape our political destinies'. They went on to say that 'this series of commemorations offers us an opportunity to explore and reflect on key episodes of our past'. What was more they promised to 'do so in a spirit of historical accuracy, mutual respect, inclusiveness and reconciliation'.[6]

We can only guess that Prime Minister Cameron did not check this speech with his education minister. Michael Gove looked at the centenary a little differently, complaining that too many academics had an 'ambiguous attitude to this country and, at worst, an unhappy compulsion on the part of some to denigrate virtues such as patriotism, honour and courage'. Gove was not interested in reconciliation with Germans, saying that

The ruthless social Darwinism of the German elites, the pitiless approach they took to occupation, their aggressively expansionist war aims and their scorn for the international order all made resistance more than justified.

No word here of the ruthless social Darwinism of British elites, nor the pitiless approach they took to occupation. According to Gove it was time to 'challenge existing Left-wing versions of the past designed to belittle Britain and its leaders'. While the Prime Minister was reassuring his Irish counterpart that now was the time to let bygones be bygones, the Education Secretary was talking up the 'bravery of men and women who fought for, and believed in, Britain's special tradition of liberty'.

Leading the Decade of Centenaries programme, Heather Humphreys struck a funereal note when she spoke at the British Legion about the war dead of 1914, discussing the 'respect that is due to the memory those who suffered'. On that level of course the Rising of 1916 is just like the Somme, or Messines Ridge –

Cause for celebration? The signing of the Ulster Covenant against Home Rule is among the many centenaries commemorated by the Irish Government

people suffered. But that really is the lowest common denominator. Suffering is not a good guide to understanding what is valuable in the past, and what is not.

The plurality of the Decade of Centenaries, by seeking to build cohesion through recognition of mutual suffering, is robbing these events of their meaning. Seen only as suffering bodies, the men and women who took part in these conflicts are being denied the motives that made them take up arms.

The difference between the Somme, Messines Ridge and the Easter Rising is that the men and women of the Easter Rising were in the right: Ireland deserved to be free; the men of the Somme were victims of a vicious blood-letting in which no-one was right, and the recruiting sergeants who led those men to their deaths, Carson and Redmond, were most decidedly in the wrong.

The Great War was not a tragedy that fell out of the sky, it was the destructive action of European statesmen, sacrificing their own people to their glory, security and wealth. The people who fought against the War in Europe, first and foremost the leaders of the Easter Rising, were those who were trying to break the power of the warmongers. Dismissing their singular and heroic action against the British War Effort as 'a direct challenge to constitutionalism and the rule of law' is the lifeless voice of conformism under tyranny.

The Decade of Centenaries group aims to handle the commemoration differently. In the past Éamon de Valera owned the 50th commemoration, making it the sanctification of his state; Liam Cosgrave tried to ban the 60th Easter Commemoration only succeeding in losing control of it; Charles Haughey clamped down on the 75th anniversary choking it. The Decade of Centenaries group has given up on trying to control the event, and chosen instead to decentre it and dilute it, by putting it alongside other events, of supposedly equal significance.

As historical study there is nothing wrong at all with the pluralistic approach. But a state that so manifestly downplays its own origins is in trouble. The Somme and the Ulster Covenant are important moments in the history of Ireland, as they are in the history of the United Kingdom and of Europe. But they are not equal in significance for the founding of the Irish state.

One sign that the Dublin government has moved too far from the sentiment of 1916 is the withdrawal of Sinn Fein from the official commemorations. Since the IRA ceasefire Sinn Fein's fortunes have lifted. In the north it became the leading nationalist party. More recently, in the south, the decline of de Valera's Fianna Fail party (mired in scandal since it was led by Charlie Haughey and losing its way under Bertie Ahern) has left the way open for a marked rise in Sinn Fein's standing as *the* nationalist party.

Sinn Fein's willingness to support the official celebrations itself was a surprise, the party having been so long outside of acceptable opinion. Now embracing the Peace Process, Sinn Fein had willingly got stuck in to the Decade of Commemorations. But the government's vapid 'Ireland Inspires' video led Sinn Fein to pull out early in 2015 and instead back an initiative called Reclaim the Vision of 1916. For that initiative, James Connolly Heron, great-grandson of the Irish Citizens Army leader, and artist Robert Ballagh have challenged the watering down of 1916 in the official commemorations. Their appeal speaks to an unmet need among Irish people for a more positive account of the rising.

The great difficulty for the elite in Ireland is that it owes the origin of its polity to the intervention of a risen people, whom today it fears. The Easter Rising is a hostage to fortune for leaders who instinctively feel they have more in common with other heads of state in Brussels than they do with the people of Ireland. The national question that so consumed Ireland – and Britain – in the years 1912–23 (and again in 1969–98) is not posed in the stark way that it was. The war is over. Partition, though, remains. The ideal of 1916 is not fulfilled and the ruling elite are managers of a divided Ireland.

Still, the spirit of Easter 1916 echoes down the century because it speaks to the determination of a people to be free and to shake off the chains that bound them. Looking out at the crowds protesting against austerity and the harsh measures demanded by the European Union and IMF, the Dublin government feels beleaguered. Are they truly the heirs to the Dáil of 1919, or of the Lord Lieutenants sent from England?

By all means, let us allow the dead to bury the dead. Life is for the living. Too much history will only bore the young who are rightly resentful of being asked to honour ancient totems. Instead we ought to find that same spirit of freedom at work in our own generation, and for century to come.

Endnotes

Introduction

1. '1916 Centenary a time for reflection not celebration', *Irish Times*, 14 January 2015
2. 'A Decade of Commemorations: Document 191', Introduction, Paragraph 3

Chapter one: History wars

1. *Irish Times*, 9 November 2013
2. *Irish Times*, 25 August 2012
3. In Jude Collins (ed), *Whose Past is it Anyway?*, Dublin, 2012, p 15
4. *Irish Times*, 9 November 2013
5. Uinsionn Mac Dubhghaill, '1916 events embarrass many now, says Lee', *Irish Times*, 18 February 1991
6. Andy Pollack, 'Twin Symbols of Loyalism and Treachery', *Irish Times*, 5 April 1991
7. Paul Bew, *Making Sense*, March 1991
8. Fintan O'Toole, 'They Fought for a Seat at the European Table', *Guardian*, 29 March 1991
9. 'The Achievement of 1916', in Owen Dudley Edwards and Fergus Pyle (eds), *1916: The Easter Rising*, Dublin, 1966, p 219; Nicholas Mansergh quoted in Diarmaid Ferriter, A Nation and Not a Rabble, London, Profile Books, 2015, p 58
10. John McGahern, 'From a Glorious Dream to a Wink and a Nod', *Irish Times*, 3 April 1991; MacGiolla, *Making Sense*, March 1991
11. Joe Carrol, '1916 commemoration opens up Pandora's box', *Irish Times*, 9 March 1991
12. Fintan O'Toole, *Guardian*, 'They Fought for a Seat at the European Table', 29 March 1991
13. *Irish Times*, 1 April 1991; notice *Irish Times* 27 March 1991

14. Quoted in Owen Dudley Edwards and Fergus Pyle (eds), *1916: The Easter Rising*, Dublin, 1966, p 115. See also the collection *1916 in 1966: Commemorating the Easter Rising*, edited by Mary Daly and Margaret Callaghan, Dublin, 2007

15. *United Irishman*, March, April and May 1966 – the march in Belfast was reportedly 80,000 strong, which seems extraordinary, though other sources put it almost as great, at 70,000.

16. 'The Embers of Easter', in Owen Dudley Edwards and Fergus Pyle (eds), *1916: The Easter Rising*, Dublin, 1966, p 225–40

17. Conor Cruise O'Brien, *States of Ireland*, London, 1972, p 150; Austen Morgan's comments in the *Observer*, 27 December 1998; John Hume's view quoted in O'Brien, *My Life and Themes*, London, 1998, p 339

18. Conor Cruise O'Brien, 'Politics and the Poet', *Irish Times*, 21 August 1975

19. Liam de Paor, 'Historical Context of the Easter Rising Analysed', *Irish Times*, 20 April 1976

20. Liam de Paor, 'The GPO Tradition', *Irish Times*, 9 March 1976

21. 'Cosgrave Coaxing Irish Support from IRA', *Guardian*, 4 March 1976

22. 'Dublin's New Ban on the Provos', *Guardian*, 22 April 1976

23. '10,000 defy ban as marchers mark Rising Anniversary', *Irish Times*, 26 April 1976; 'IRA Defies Ban on Dublin March', *New York Times*, 26 April 1976

24. Quoted in Colm Tobin, 'Playboys of the GPO', *London Review of Books*, Vol. 18 No. 8, 18 April 1996

Chapter two: The Rising in history

1. A. L. Morton and George Tate, *The British Labour Movement*, London, 1979, p 254

2. Lajpat Rai, *Young India*, London, 1917, p 137

3. Alfred Cobban, *A History of Modern France, 1871–1962*, London, 1965, p 97

4. R. J. Crampton, *The Hollow Détente – Anglo-German Relations in the Balkans*, London, George Prior, 1979, p 7

5. William Manchester, *The Arms of Krupp*, Boston, 2003, p 266

6. *The Nation*, August 15, 1914

7. Jack London, *People of the Abyss*, London, 1992, p 61

8. David Lloyd George, *War Memoirs*, Volume I, Boston, 1937, p 34–40

9. D. R. O'Connor Lysaght, 'British Imperialism in Ireland', in Morgan and Purdie, *Ireland: Divided Nation; Divided Class*, London, 1980, p 17

10. C. Desmond Greaves, *Liam Mellows*, London, 1988, p 14

11. In Canning, *British Policy Towards Ireland, 1921–1941*, Oxford, 1985, p 156

12. Michael Farrell, *The Orange State*, London, 1983, p 18

13. Austen Morgan, *Labour and Partition*, London, 1991, p 11

14. Thomas Dooley, *Irishmen of English Soldiers*, Liverpool, 1995, p 38

15. George Dangerfield, *The Damnable Question*, London, 1979, p 86

16. Dangerfield, *The Damnable Question*, p 127

17. Lewis Namier, *Vanished supremacies*, New York, 1963, p 167

18. Max Hastings, *Catastrophe*, London, 2014, p 9

19. Russell, *The Nation*, 15 August 1914; Nan Milton, *John Maclean*, London, 1973, p 81

20. Lloyd George, *War Memoirs*, Volume I, Boston, 1937, p 65, 67

21. Robin Wilson, 'Imperialism in Crisis', in M. Langan and B. Schwarz, *Crises in the British State 1880–1930*, London, 1985, p 164

22. Cobban, *History of Modern France*, London, 1965, p 108

23. Ruth Dudley Edwards, *James Connolly*, Dublin, 1981, p 120

24. Jane Leonard, 'The catholic chaplaincy', in David Fitzpatrick (ed) *Ireland and the First World War*, Dublin, 1986, p 3

25. Dangerfield, *The Damnable Question*, London, 1979, p 134

26. Dooley, *Irishmen or English Soldiers*, Liverpool, 1995, p 197

27. Dooley, *Irishmen or English Soldiers*, p 7
28. David Lloyd George, *War Memoirs*, Vol II, Boston, 1937, p 696
29. Dooley, *Irishmen or English Soldiers*, p 196
30. Dangerfield, *The Damnable Question*, p 132; Ulster Volunteer Force, *Souvenir Booklet 1912–2002*, Belfast, 2002, p 31
31. Uinsionn Mac Dubhghaill, '1916 events embarrass many now, says Lee', *Irish Times*, 18 February 1991
32. Ulster Volunteer Force, *Souvenir Booklet 1912–2002*, Belfast, 2002, p 32
33. Paul Frölich, *Rosa Luxemburg*, Chicago, 2010, p 221
34. Richard Doherty, *The Sons of Ulster*, Appletree Press, 1992, p 18, 21
35. Ulster Volunteer Force, *Souvenir Booklet 1912–2002*, Belfast, 2002, p 11
36. Richard Doherty, *The Sons of Ulster*, Belfast, 1992, p 24
37. Jean and Desmond Bowen, *Heroic Option*, Barnsley, 2005, p 287
38. Martin Staunton, *Royal Munster Fusiliers in the Great War*, University College Dublin Thesis, 1986, p 64–5
39. Nan Milton, *John Maclean*, London, 1973, p 129
40. *Workers' Republic*, 15 April 1916
41. 'MacNeill on the Easter Rising', *Irish Historical Studies*, March 1961, p 234
42. Dangerfield, *The Damnable Question*, London, 1979, p 216
43. Dangerfield, *The Damnable Question*, p 209
44. J. C. Lee, *Ireland, 1912–1985*, Cambridge UP, 1990

Chapter three: A shot that echoed around the world

1. Luke Gibbon's talk, 'Recasting the Rising: 1916 on the World Stage', at the Theatre of War Symposium, 22 January 2015 at the Abbey Theatre, touches on many of the connections covered in this chapter.
2. 4 May 1916, quoted in David Ayerst, *The Manchester*

Guardian, Ithaca 1971, p 392

3. David Lloyd George, *War Memoirs*, Vol II, Boston, 1937, p 703

4. In 1921, quoted in Judith Brown and William Roger Louis (eds), *Oxford History of the British Empire*, Vol IV, Oxford, 2001, p 146

5. Liam Cahill, *Forgotten Revolution*, Dublin, 1990, p 18

6. Charles Townshend, *The British Campaign in Ireland 1919–1921*, London, 1975, p 9, 10

7. *Nottingham Evening Post*, 31 December 1918; *Aberdeen Journal*, 13 January 1919

8. Liam Cahill, *The Forgotten Revolution*, Dublin, 1990

9. Richard Holmes, *The Little Field Marshal: A Life of Sir John French*, London, 2005, p 356–7

10. D M Leeson, *The Black and Tans*, Oxford, 2011, p 1, 15, 24–5; Heartfield, *Unpatriotic History of the Second World War*, Alresford, 2012, p 149

11. *Yorkshire Post and Leeds Intelligencer*, 2 April 1934; *Western Morning News*, 26 March 1940

12. *Manchester Guardian*, 11 June 1932; Paul Canning, *British Policy Towards Ireland 1921–1941*, Oxford, 1985, p 128, 133

13. Paul Canning, *British Policy Towards Ireland 1921–1941*, Oxford, 1985, p 246, 299

14. *Sunday Post*, 12 January 1919

15. *Daily Herald*, 2 December 1916

16. John MacLean, *The Irish Tragedy*, Glasgow, 1970 [orig. 1920], with an introduction by Harry MacShane; Nan Milton, *John Maclean*, London, 1973, p 129

17. Minutes of the Second Congress of the Communist International, Fourth Session, 25 July; Executive Committee, Communist Party of Great Britain, *The Communist*, 25 November 1920; Paul Canning, *British Policy Towards Ireland 1921–1941*, Oxford, 1985, p 88

18. T. A. Jackson, *Ireland Her Own*, London, 1991, p 401; Executive Committee, Communist Party of Great Britain, *The*

Communist, November 25, 1920

19. Austen Morgan, *Labour and Partition,* London, 1991, p 235, 238, 240, 249

20. Conor Kostick, *Revolution in Ireland: Popular militancy 1917 to 1923,* London, 1996, p 154–5

21. C.L.R. James, as 'J.R. Johnson', 'Ireland and the Revolutionary Tradition of Easter Week,' *Labor Action,* Vol. 5 No. 14, 14 April 1941, p. 3; Leon Trotsky, *The First Five Years of the Communist International,* Volume 1, New York, 2009, p 169

22. http://blogs.channel4.com/paul-mason-blog/world-war/1240

23. Liam Cahill, *Forgotten Revolution,* Dublin, 1990, p 22

24. Tom Barry, *Guerilla Days in Ireland,* Dublin, 1981, p 1–5

25. Dooley, *Irishmen or English Soldiers,* Liverpool, 1995, p 164

26. The story is told in Michael Sivestri's *Ireland and India: Nationalism, Memory and Empire,* Cambridge, 2009, pp 139–46; and also in Anthony Babington's *The Devil To Pay,* London, 1991

27. Julian Putkowski, *British Army Mutineers, 1914–1922,* London, 1998, p 13

28. Nan Milton, *John McLean,* London, 1973, p 197

29. Michael Silvestri, *Ireland and India,* Cambridge 2009, p 52, 27, 36, 35, 28, 47, 60, 62, 58, 229, 52

30. C. A. Bayly and Tim Harper, *Forgotten Armies: Britain's Asian Empire & War with Japan,* London, 2005, p 11, 9

31. Pierre Brocheux, *Ho Chi Minh,* Camridge, 2007, p 10; Tran Dan Tien, *Ho Chi Minh,* Hanoi, 1989, p 10

32. Elizabeth Keane, *Sean MacBride,* Dublin, 2007, p 52; T. Ryle Dwyer, *De Valera,* Dublin, 1991, p 47

33. Sam Nujoma, *Where Others Wavered,* London, 2001, p 220, 257

34. Kader Asmal, *Politics in My Blood,* Ithaca, 2011, p 51, 65

35. Colin Grant, *Negro With a Hat,* London, 2009, p 198; Michael Silvestri, Ireland and India, Cambridge, 2009, p 31; 'Program

of the African Blood Brotherhood', *Communist Review* [London], v. 2, no. 6 (April 1922), p 449–54

36. John Gallagher, 'Nationalisms and the Crisis of Empire', *Modern Asian Studies*, Vol 15, No 3, 1981, p 362; *Irish Times*, 1 April 1930

37. Deirdre McMahon, 'Ireland and the Empire', in *Oxford History of the British Empire*, vol. IV (eds Judith Brown and Wm. Roger Louis), Oxford, 2001, p 149

38. Richard Davis, *Irish Issues in New Zealand Politics*, Dunedin, 1974, p 189–202; Deirdre McMahon, 'Ireland and the Empire', in *Oxford History of the British Empire*, vol. IV (eds Judith Brown and Wm. Roger Louis), Oxford, 2001, p 149

39. See T. Ryle Dwyer, *De Valera*, Dublin, 1991, chapter four

Chapter four: Revising the Rising

1. Ruth Dudley Edwards, *Patrick Pearse: The Triumph of Failure*, London, 1977, p 326–7, 343, 173, 179, 337–8; Liam de Paor in 'Historical Context of Easter Rising Analysed', *Irish Times*, 20 April 1976

2. http://www.ruthdudleyedwards.co.uk/nonfiction/Pearse-Irtimes-article.html

3. Owen Dudley Edwards, *Éamon de Valera*, Cardiff, 1987, p 48

4. Austen Morgan, *James Connolly – A political biography*, Manchester, 1988, p 199; but compare Ann Matthews, The Irish Citizen Army, Mercier Press, 2014, for a more balanced view.

5. Austen Morgan, *James Connolly*, p 45

6. Austen Morgan, *James Connolly*, p 35

7. Austen Morgan, *James Connolly*, p 37, 210

8. Austen Morgan, *James Connolly*, p 23, 17

9. Austen Morgan, *James Connolly*, p 11; Lenin, 'The Discussion On Self-Determination Summed Up', section 10, https://www.marxists.org/archive/lenin/works/1916/jul/x01.htm

10. Austen Morgan, *James Connolly*, p 159

11. Roy Foster, *Vivid Faces*, London, Allen Lane, 2014, pp 111, 116, 96–7, 26, 72–3

12. Austen Morgan, *Labour and Partition*, London, 1991, p 317

13. Austen Morgan and Bob Purdie (eds), *Ireland: Divided Nation; Divided Class*, London, 1980, p 153

14. Morgan and Purdie, *Ireland: Divided Nation; Divided Class*, p 154

15. Morgan and Purdie, *Ireland: Divided Nation; Divided Class*, p 159

16. Austen Morgan, *Labour and Partition*, London, 1991, p xvi

17. Michael Farrell, *The Orange State*, London, 1976, p 16, 291–2; Paul Bew in *Ireland: Divided Nation, Divided Class*, 1980, p 157–8; and see Eric Hobsbawm's essay 'The Aristocracy of Labour in Nineteenth Century Britain', in *Labouring Men*, London, 1972

18. Henry Patterson and Eric Kaufmann, *Unionism and Orangeism in Northern Ireland Since 1945*, Manchester, 2007, pp 10, 44

19. Austen Morgan and Bob Purdie (eds), *Ireland: Divided Nation; Divided Class*, London, 1980, p 170

20. Brian Hanley and Scott Millar, *The Lost Revolution: The Official IRA and the Workers Party*, Dublin, p 387

21. Henry Patterson, 'The State of Marxism in Ireland', *Class Politics Journal*, 1983, p 4–7; Austen Morgan 'Northern Ireland Terrorism: the Legal Response' in James Dingley, *Combating Terrorism in Northern Ireland*, London Routledge, 2009, p 171–3

22. Owen Dudley Edwards, *The Sins of Our Fathers*, Dublin, 1970, ix; Roy Foster, *Modern Ireland*, London, 1989, p 595

23. Michael Tierney, *Eoin MacNeill, Scholar and Man of Action*, Oxford, 1980, p 369, 269

24. Roy Foster, *Modern Ireland*, p 595

25. Owen Dudley Edwards, *Éamon de Valera*, Cardiff, 1987, p 12; Paul Bew, Ellen Hazelkorn, Henry Patterson, *The Dynamics of*

Irish Politics, London, 1989, p 82

26. R. F. Foster, *Vivid Faces*, Allen Lane, 2014, p 117

27. 'Too much history' – see for example Kevin Toolis' preface to *Rebel Hearts*, London, 1996; Leopold Amery quoted in Judith Brown and William Roger Louis (eds), *Oxford History of the British Empire*, Vol IV, Oxford, 2001, p 159; Margaret Thatcher, *The Downing Street Years*, London, 1995, p 400

28. *Times*, 8 September 1971

29. *Times*, 26 April 1972; Fintan O'Toole, 'Easter Charade', *Observer*, 7 April 1996

Chapter five: Historical memory and the peace process

1. Ann Marie Gray and Derek Birrell, 'Coalition Government in Northern Ireland: Social Policy and the Lowest Common Denominator Thesis', *Social Policy and Society*, 11, 2012, p 15–25

2. Beatrix Campbell, *Agreement*, London, 2008, p 185

3. *Report of the Consultative Group on the Past*, p 49–54

4. Kathryn Stone, 'Dealing with the past: "There must never be a hierarchy of pain"', *Open Democracy*, 2 June 2014, https://www.opendemocracy.net/5050/kathryn-stone/dealing-with-past-there-must-never-be-hierarchy-of-pain

5. http://www.taoiseach.gov.ie/eng/Historical_Information/1916_Commemorations/#sthash.ZLVcQ8kG.dpuf

6. http://www.huffingtonpost.co.uk/2012/03/12/david-cameron-and-enda-kenny-statement-full-text_n_1339029.html. There is a good discussion of these themes in the collection *Ireland's 1916 Rising: Explorations of History-Making, Commemoration & Heritage in Modern Times*, edited by Mark McCarthy, Ashgate, 2013

Contemporary culture has eliminated both the concept of the public and the figure of the intellectual. Former public spaces – both physical and cultural – are now either derelict or colonized by advertising. A cretinous anti-intellectualism presides, cheerled by expensively educated hacks in the pay of multinational corporations who reassure their bored readers that there is no need to rouse themselves from their interpassive stupor. The informal censorship internalized and propagated by the cultural workers of late capitalism generates a banal conformity that the propaganda chiefs of Stalinism could only ever have dreamt of imposing. Zer0 Books knows that another kind of discourse – intellectual without being academic, popular without being populist – is not only possible: it is already flourishing, in the regions beyond the striplit malls of so-called mass media and the neurotically bureaucratic halls of the academy. Zer0 is committed to the idea of publishing as a making public of the intellectual. It is convinced that in the unthinking, blandly consensual culture in which we live, critical and engaged theoretical reflection is more important than ever before.